Thunder in the Heavens

CLASSIC AMERICAN AIRCRAFT OF WORLD WAR II

Thunder in the Heavens

CLASSIC AMERICAN AIRCRAFT OF WORLD WAR II

STRATHEARN BOOKS LIMITED
Toronto, Canada

A Salamander Book

This edition published by
STRATHEARN BOOKS LIMITED
Toronto. Canada

© Salamander Books Ltd 1994

ISBN 0 86288 232 X

All correspondence concerning
the content of this volume
should be addressed to
Salamander Books Ltd.

Editor: Christopher Westhorp
Designer: Paul Johnson
Color artwork: © Pilot Press Ltd.
and © Salamander Books Ltd.
Filmset by SX Composing Ltd.
Color Reproduction by
P & W Graphics PTE Ltd, Singapore

Printed and bound in Italy

Credits

Unless stated otherwise, the quoted material in this book is the product of interviews or exchanges of correspondence with the author. The publishers would like to express their gratitude to all the contributors named in the book. Every effort has been made to trace the holders of published, copyrighted material quoted and that which appears does so courtesy of the respective copyright holders, where known. The sources are as follows: **Page 12,** *The Combat Record of T.Sgt. Donald V. Chase,* unpublished memoirs. **Page 14,** *The Flight from Boyhood* by T. Sgt. Robert T. Marshall, unpublished manuscript. **Pages 16-17** and **18-19,** *Chick's Crew* by Ben Smith Jr, published privately 1978. **Page 22,** *The Tibbets' Story* by Paul W. Tibbets, Clair C. Stebbins and Harry Franken, Stein & Day, New York 1978. **Page 24,** *Kangaroo Squadron – Memories of a Pacific Bomber Pilot* by Lt. Col. John Wallace Fields, published privately 1982. **Page 25,** *Grey Goose Calling: A History of the 11th Bomb Group* edited by W. M. Cleveland, published by 11th Bomb Group Association, 1981. **Page 26,** Sgt. Maynard Smith's Medal of Honor Citation. **Page 29,** *Chick's Crew,* 1978. **Page 31,** *Flying Magazine,* October 1943. **Page 44,** *Kangaroo Squadron,* 1982. **Page 45,** *Experiences of a World War II Navigator* by John W. McClane, published privately 1985. **Page 52,** *High Honor: Recollections of Men and Women of World War II Aviation* by Stuart Leuthner and Oliver Jensen, Smithsonian Institution Press, Washington DC 1989, pages 189-190. **Page 54,** *Superfortress: The B-29 & American Air Power* by Maj. Gen. Curtis E. LeMay & Bill Yenne, McGraw Hill, New York 1988. **Page 55** (left), *High Honor,* Washington DC 1989, pages 189-190. **Page 55** (right), *Day of the Bomb: Hiroshima 1945* by Dan Kurzman, Weidenfeld & Nicolson, London 1986. **Page 56,** *Yank* magazine, 7 September 1945. **Page 57** (left), *The Tibbets' Story,* New York 1978. **Page 57** (right) *Day of the Bomb,* London 1986. **Page 58** (left), *Day of the Bomb,* London 1986. **Page 58** (right), *Experiences of a World War II Navigator,* 1985. **Page 59,** *Day of the Bomb,* London 1986. **Page 60** (top), author interview with Abe Dolim. **Page 60** (center), *Bomber Pilot* by Eino Alve, published

privately 1988. **Page 62** (top), *Flying Buccaneers* by Steve Birdsall, David & Charles, London 1977. **Page 62** (bottom), *High Honor,* Washington DC 1989, page 161. **Page 64** (left), *Fighter Command: American Fighters in Color* by Jeffrey L. Ethell and Robert T. Sand, Motorbooks International, Minnesota 1991. **Page 66,** *Experiences of a World War II Navigator,* 1985. **Page 67,** *Brief History of the 25th Bomb Group* by George R. Sesler, published privately, year unknown. **Pages 68-69,** *Happy Jack's Go Buggy* by Jack Ilfrey, Exposition Press, Hicksville NY 1979. **Pages 70-71,** *Dick Bong: Ace of Aces* by Gen. George C. Kenney, Duell, Sloan & Pierce Inc., New York 1960. **Page 72** (top), *Flying Tiger: Chennault of China* by Robert Lee Scott Jr, Doubleday & Co, Inc., New York 1959. *Page 72* (center and bottom), *High Honor,* Washington DC 1989, page 28. **Page 74** (left), *Flying Tiger,* New York 1959. **Page 74** (right), *High Honor,* Washington DC 1989, page 32. **Page 75,** *Flying Magazine,* October 1943. **Pages 76-77,** *Flying Tiger,* New York 1959. **Page 80** (left), *Flying Magazine,* February 1944. **Page 82** (left), *Nanette* by Lt. Edwards Park, Smithsonian Institution Press, Washington DC 1977. **Pages 82** (right)-**83,** *Air Force* magazine, February 1944. **Pages 86-87.** *Lion in the Sky: US 8th Air Force Fighter Operations 1942-45* by Jerry Scutts, Patrick Stephens Limited, Sparkford, Somerset 1987. **Page 88** (left) *Nanette,* Washington DC 1977. **Page 88** (right), *Fighter Command,* Motorbooks International, Minnesota 1991. **Page 89** (left), *Yeager* by Gen. Chuck Yeager & Leo Janos, Bantam, New York 1985. **Page 89** (right) *Combat Encounter Report* by Maj. John B. England, via Robert M. Foose. **Pages 90-91,** *Lion in the Sky,* Somerset 1987. **Pages 92-93,** *High Honor,* Washington DC 1989, page 193. **Page 94,** *Air Force* magazine, February 1944. **Page 96,** *Yank* magazine, April 1942. **Page 99,** *Air Force* magazine, February 1944. **Page 102** (center and bottom), *High Honor,* Washington DC 1989, pages 161-162. **Page 104,** *Target Germany,* His Majesty's Stationery Office (HMSO), London

1944. **Page 105,** *High Honor,* Washington DC 1989. **Page 106,** Martin Aircraft press release, August 1943. **Page 107,** *Brief History of the 25th Bomb Group.* **Page 114,** *High Honor,* Washington DC 1989, page 43. **Page 116,** *Five at a Clip* by Stanley Johnston, publisher and year unknown. **Page 118,** *Into the Drink* by Maj. Joe Foss, publisher and year unknown. **Page 121,** *Aerial Combat Escapades: A Pilot's Logbook* by Maj. J. Hunter Reinberg, GCBA Publishing, Grand

Canyon, Arizona 1988. **Page 122,** *Baa Baa Black Sheep* by Gregory Boyington, The Putnam Berkley Group, Inc., New York 1958. **Pages 124-125** and **127,** *Aerial Combat Escapades,* 1988. **Page 128,** *High Honor,* Washington DC 1989, page 43. **Page 131,** *Battle over Palembang,* by Hideaki Inayama, publisher and year unknown. **Page 132,** *High Honor,* Washington DC 1989, page 43. **Page 133,** *High Honor,* Washington DC 1989, page 83. **Page 134,** *Kamikaze* by Yasuo Kuwahara & Gordon T. Allred, Ballantine Books Inc., New York 1957. **Page 136,** *Hellcat: The F6F in World War II* by Barrett Tillman, US Naval Institute Press, Annapolis 1979, page 29. **Page 139,** *High Honor,* Washington DC 1989, page 57.

In Memory of Paddy

Page 1: B-24 Liberator, B-17 Flying Fortress (above)
2/3: B-24 Liberator, B-17 Flying Fortress
4/5: P-51 Mustangs
6/7: B-24 Liberator
8: B-17 Flying Fortress
9: B-24 Liberator, F4F Wildcat
10: B-25 Mitchell's gun
11: B-17 Flying Fortress (left); P-51 Mustang, P-38 Lightning (top)

Contents

The potential of aircraft as formidable weapons of war was proved during World War I and by the 1920s visionaries, such as American Brig. Gen. William "Billy" Mitchell, could foresee a day when the bomber would render the battleship obsolete. So forcibly did he pursue his belief – that aerial bombardment would become the most important instrument of war – that he was court-martialed in 1925 and forced to resign on 1 February 1926. Fifteen years later, on 7 December 1941, Mitchell's prophecy came true when the United States suffered a massive blow in the form of the Japanese air attack on Pearl Harbor in the Hawaiian islands. Eight battleships and three cruisers were among the damaged and sunken ships of the US Pacific Fleet, and more than 2,000 sailors, soldiers and airmen perished.

Aircraft destroyed on the ground at Hickam Field included a specially modified Consolidated B-24A ready for an armed reconnaissance of Japanese installations in the Marshall and Caroline islands. The United States Army Air Force (USAAF), previously the United States Army Air Corps (USAAC), repossessed 15 B-24As destined for Britain's Royal Air Force (RAF) and dispatched them to the Pacific but none reached the Philippines before the Japanese occupied the islands. On 16 January 1942 three LB-30s and two B-17s from the 7th Bomb Group (BG) at Singosari, Malang, carried out the first Liberator action of the war by USAAF crews with a raid on Japanese shipping and airfields.

Big Friends
On 2 April 1942 the 10th Air Force (AF) in the China–Burma–India (CBI) theater, equipped with a few B-17s and B-24s, flew its first mission with an attack on the Andaman Islands. Early in the war the US Navy recognized the need for a long-range, land-based, patrol aircraft. By July 1942 the USAAF had agreed to the US Navy receiving a quantity of B-24s, which were named PB4Y-1s; it was without doubt the finest patrol bomber of the war. On land, in March 1943 Liberators in the 308th BG joined Gen. Claire L. Chennault's China Task Force (later 14th AF). The 308th BG flew its first mission from China in May 1943.

B-17 Flying Fortress missions began from England on 17 August 1942 and later the first Liberators joined them on raids over Europe. The first mission to Germany was flown on 27 January 1943 when 55 B-17s hit shipyards at Vegasack and Emden. B-17s and B-24s were the most famous heavy bombers in the strategic bombing offensive in Europe, or the "Big League" as it was known. One of the most famous raids was made from Libya on 1 August 1943 by 167 B-24D Liberators of the 8th and 9th AFs on Romanian oil fields at Ploesti. Some 311 tons of bombs were dropped on the refineries and 42% of Ploesti's refining capacity and 40% of its cracking capacity were destroyed for the loss of 57 B-24Ds. Five Medals of Honor (three posthumously) were awarded, and all five participating groups received Presidential Unit Citations.

From 1942 to 1945 the 8th AF in England, and the 12th and 15th AFs in the Mediterranean, waged an almost daily assault on the Reich. On 17 August 1943 the 8th AF made simultaneous strikes on aircraft plants at Schweinfurt and Regensburg, losing 60 B-17s. A further 88 B-17s were lost during 8-10 October and on 14 October. Sixty more, or 19% of the force, were then lost on a further raid on Schweinfurt and 142 of the 231 bombers that returned were damaged. From November all new Fortress groups were equipped with the B-17G with a "chin turret" to improve forward defense. Although the 8th AF's 3rd Bomb Division (BD) converted from the B-24 to the B-17, there were not enough Fortresses to equip all three divisions and the 2nd BD flew Liberators until the end of the war. Five factories in the United States produced 18,188 Liberators – more than any other American aircraft of the period.

In the Mediterranean theater Gen. Henry H. Arnold changed the 12th AF into a tactical organization and on 1 November 1943 created the 15th AF with 90 B-24s and 210 B-17s. On 5 January 1944 the 8th AF in England and the 15th

AF in Italy merged to form the US Strategic Air Forces under Gen. Carl Spaatz. A series of strikes on the German aircraft industry during 20-25 February 1944 became known as "Big Week" and it cost Spaatz 226 bombers. On 4 March 1944 B-17s of the 8th AF dropped the first American bombs on Berlin. In April overall command of the combined bomber offensive was officially assumed by Gen. Dwight D. Eisenhower, the Supreme Allied Commander, Allied Expeditionary Forces (SHAEF). Bomber attacks in support of the coming invasion of Europe began in February with raids on French rail junctions, airfields, ports and bridges. On D-Day, 6 June 1944, Liberators led the first of three strikes on the Normandy and Cherbourg invasion areas. Altogether, 2,362 bomber sorties were flown on D-Day for the loss of only three B-24s.

By June 1944 the 15th AF was bombing railway networks in southeast Europe in support of Russian military operations in Romania. On 2 June the 15th AF flew its first "shuttle" mission when 130 B-17s and P-51 escorts landed in Russia after a raid on Hungary. Two more 15th AF "shuttle" missions followed and then on 21 June the 8th AF flew the first of two "shuttle" missions, bombing Berlin and landing at Poltava, Russia, only to have 43 B-17s and several P-51s destroyed in an audacious Luftwaffe attack. In July the 15th AF hit some targets in southern France in a prelude to the

Operation Anvil/Dragoon invasion. During late 1944-early 1945 mighty fleets of 8th and 15th AF bombers hit oil refineries in Germany, Czechoslovakia and Romania. On Christmas Eve a record 2,034 8th AF bombers took part in the largest single strike by the Allied air forces in the war, to help relieve America troops in the Battle of the Bulge in the Ardennes.

On 18 March 1945 a record 1,327 8th AF bombers raided Berlin and on 23/24 March the Allied armies crossed the Rhine supported by 1,747 aircraft and hundreds of transports and B-24 Liberators which dropped supplies by parachute. On 8 April the 8th AF sent 32 heavy bomber and 14 Mustang groups to Germany. A week later the largest 15th AF operation of the war took place when 1,235 bombers bombed targets near Bologna. The last major air battle in Europe occurred on 18 April when 1,211 bombers, escorted by more than 1,200 fighters, raided Berlin. Forty Me 262s used rockets to shoot down 25 bombers but it was a last gasp – V-weapon sites were overrun, while lack of fuel and suitable pilots had virtually driven the Luftwaffe from the skies. In the first week of May Germany surrendered.

Meanwhile, the war in the Far East and Pacific theaters dragged on, with some four strategic air forces committed. In September 1944 the 5th and 13th AFs, collectively known as the Far East Air Force, had begun making attacks on the

Philippines and supporting the island-hopping campaign across the Pacific. From August 1944 until 19 February 1945 7th AF Liberators in the Pacific flew strikes against Iwo Jima and surrounding islands. The first 20th AF mission with B-29 Superfortresses had taken place on 5 June 1944 when landing fields in China were used as staging posts to refuel and rearm 98 B-29s based in India for the 2,000-mile (3,200km) round trip to bomb rail targets in Bangkok. On 15/16 June the first raid on the Japanese mainland occurred when 47 B-29s made a night attack on the Imperial Iron and Steel Works at Yawata on the island of Kyushu; seven B-29s were lost. In August 1944 the longest mission of the war for a B-29 took place with a 3,950-mile (6,350km) flight from Ceylon to Palembang in Sumatra.

From late 1944 all B-29s of XXI Bomber Command (BC), 20th AF, were based at five airfields in the Marianas. On 24 November 1944 Brig. Gen. Rosie O'Donnell's 73rd Wing made the first B-29 raid on Tokyo, bombing the Musashima aircraft factory. Throughout late 1944 and early 1945 B-29s carried out high-level daylight raids with high losses and little success. In March 1945 Maj. Gen. Curtis E. LeMay, who had arrived in the CBI theater to take command of XX BC, 20th AF, in August 1944, switched the B-29s to area bombing using incendiaries to burn large areas of Japanese cities, a technique he had employed successfully in the European Theater of Operations (ETO) with the 8th AF.

On the night of 9/10 March over 300 B-29s, each carrying 8 tons of M69 incendiaries to drop to the pattern set by the fires started by pathfinders, fire-bombed Tokyo at heights ranging from 4,900 to 9,200ft (1,500-2,800m). Almost 16 sq miles (41 sq km) of the city were razed to the ground and over 80,000 Japanese died; 14 B-29s were lost and 42 received flak damage. LeMay scheduled a further five fire-bomb missions in 10 days. By April 1945 he had four wings and up to 700 Superfortresses under his command but Japan refused to concede defeat.

Little Friends

The "heavies" were accompanied on their bombing raids by close escort fighters. It was a far cry from before the United States' entry into the war, when Gen. Chennault's American Volunteer Group (AVG) had fought on the Chinese Nationalist side flying P-40 Warhawks. Never a match in dogfights with the nimble Zero, by using hit-and-run tactics they nevertheless destroyed 286 Japanese aircraft. Another famous fighter which saw early action in the Pacific (and Europe) was the P-38 Lightning, which was already in mass production before the outbreak of hostilities. Originally designed in 1937 as a high-altitude interceptor, it was put to good use as a strike aircraft and as a long-range escort in the Pacific and European theaters protecting American "heavies" on deep-penetration missions.

The P-38 entered combat on 15 October 1942 with the 55th Fighter Group (FG), equipped with the longer range P-38H Lightning. Beginning in November 1942 P-38s also saw large-scale service in North Africa and the Mediterranean theater. Based in England, the 9th Tactical AF operated three fighter groups, and of them the 374th used P-38s until the end of the war. When production ceased in 1945 9,535 P-38 fighters had been built.

During late 1944 five P-38 groups re-equipped with the P-51 Mustang and one with the P-47 Thunderbolt. In February 1943 both the 56th and 78th FGs of the 8th AF were operational on the P-47C and P-47D, but teething troubles postponed their debut until 13 April. Despite weighing twice that of any other single-engine fighter, the P-47 could climb to 15,000ft (4,600m) in six minutes and dive on enemy formations from above 30,000ft (9,150m) at 504mph (811kph). It was popularly known, therefore, as "Jug" (for Juggernaut) because of its ability to outdive any other fighter. The 56th FG was unique in the 8th AF because it retained its P-47s until the end of hostilities. Many famous aces served with this unit, including its commanding officer Col. Hubert Zemke (17¾ confirmed victories in the air), Maj. Gerald W. Johnson (with 18 victories), and the top scoring fighter aces, Col. Francis "Gabby" Gabreski (who was the leading ace in the ETO with 28 victories and 2½ strafing credits) and Maj. Robert Johnson (28 victories).

The greatest fighter of the war was the North American P-51 Mustang, which saw widespread use as an escort fighter on deep-penetration raids. By the end of the war the P-51 equipped all but one of the 8th AF fighter groups. On 14 January 1945 Mustangs of the 8th AF destroyed 161 enemy aircraft. The 357th FG, which finished the war with 38 aces, shot down 60½ enemy aircraft, a record for any 8th AF fighter group and one that still stood by the end of the hostilities in Europe. On 10 April 1945 some 297 German aircraft were strafed and destroyed, and on 16 April just over 700 aircraft were destroyed on the ground. A few P-51Hs, the fastest of all the models, reached the Pacific theater before the end of the war and served operationally. Altogether, 15,586 versions of the Mustang were built.

Low and Below
North American also built the finest medium bomber of the war. The B-25 Mitchell was designed in 1934 as a light, fast attack bomber, but by 1940 had developed into a medium as a result of a United States Army Air Corps (USAAC) requirement in 1938. North American built a prototype as a private venture and in September 1939 the USAAC ordered 184 B-25s, the first of them flying on 19 August 1940. Its contemporary, the Martin B-26 Marauder, was designed to a specification issued by the USAAC on 25 January 1939. On 5 July the Martin 179 design beat competing designs and 201 B-26As were ordered in September without the benefit of prototypes or testing. The first B-26 was flown on 25 November 1940 with mixed results – a high landing speed, and an increase in gross weight on the B-26A, resulting in many accidents during early test and training flights.

When the United States entered the war, medium

bombers were among the first to see action. During an anti-shipping strike off the west coast of the USA on 24 December 1941, a B-25A of the 17th BG sank a Japanese submarine. On 8 December 1941, 53 of the first 56 B-26A Marauders had taken off from Langley Field, Virginia, for Australia where they formed the 22nd BG. In April 1942 B-26As of the 22nd BG and B-25B Mitchells of the 3rd BG entered combat against the Japanese. On 18 April 1942 Lt. Col. (later Gen.) James H Doolittle earned a Medal of Honor for leading an audacious strike by 16 B-25Bs from the carrier USS *Hornet* while it lay at sea some 823 miles (1,324km) from the targets in Tokyo and three other cities. Most crash-landed safely in China, but several crews were captured and three airmen were executed by the Japanese. Bomb loads were, of necessity, small, but news of the "Tokyo Raiders" boosted morale and prompted the Japanese to plan counter-attacks on the US fleet.

The Douglas A-26 Invader had been designed in January 1941 as a replacement for the A-20 and in July 1942 it flew for the first time. The A-26 was ordered for trials by the US Army for use as an attack bomber and, in another configuration, as a night fighter but production was slow. It finally entered combat in September 1944 when 18 A-26s attacked Brest. It had proved a powerful offensive weapon. It also served in Italy and the Pacific as a fighter-bomber in the 5th and 7th AFs.

In spring 1943 B-26 Marauders began equipping the 322nd BG, 8th AF, in Suffolk, England, for low-level operations. The first mission, to Holland on 14 May, went well, but on 17 May all 10 attacking B-26s were shot down. The Marauder force was quickly allocated bases in Essex so as to place them nearer the continent and thus within the flying range of escort fighters. During the summer of 1943 Marauders were switched to a medium-level bombing role escorted in tight box formations by large numbers of RAF Spitfires. On 16 October 1943 all four 8th AF B-26 groups were transferred to the 9th AF for tactical missions in support of the invasion of Europe.

The Mitchell was thought better suited to the Pacific island-hopping campaign than the B-26, which was therefore replaced in February 1944 by the B-25H. North American built 405 B-25Gs and 1,000 B-25Hs (248 B-25H models were transferred to the United States Marine Corps). Both packed a "solid" nose containing a 75mm cannon for use against shipping and ground targets but only four shells could be fired on a single run, and on many B-25s the gun was replaced by two 0.50in caliber machine guns. The B-25J, introduced in August 1944, returned to a transparent nose and with 12 0.50in caliber fixed guns, plus six hand-held guns, was the most heavily armed aircraft of its size in the US air forces. The majority fought in the southwest Pacific where Mitchells became famous for "masthead" and "skip-bombing" strikes.

By May 1944 the 9th AF commanded eight Marauder groups and a pathfinder squadron. On D-Day, 6 June, a total of 742 B-26 sorties were flown in support of Operation Overlord. On 3 May 1945 a force of 126 A-26s and eight PFF B-26 Marauders flew the final 9th AF mission of the war against the Stod Ammon plant, Czechoslovakia. In total, some 5,266 Marauders were built and 2,446 A-26 Invaders. The A-26 proved to be the last propeller-driven, twin-engined bomber in production for the USAAF. It entered the war late in 1944 and proved itself a powerful offensive weapon, flying 11,567 sorties in Europe and continuing in service in the Pacific until the end of World War II and beyond.

Flying from the Flat Tops

The US Navy bore much of the responsibility for ensuring Allied air superiority was regained in the nearly 64 million sq miles (165 million sq km) of the Pacific Ocean. Almost 20 naval battles involving the US Navy and the Imperial Japanese Navy were fought during 1941-45 and five of them were fought between aircraft carriers. US Navy fighter squadrons flew, among others, the Grumman F4F-3 Wildcat. On 8 December 1941 the first Wildcats to see action were United States Marine Corps' (USMC) F4F-3s of VMF-211, making up the defenses of Wake Island. Although slower than other American fighters, and outperformed by the Mitsubishi Zero, in the Pacific theater the Wildcat was to average a near 7:1 ratio of kills, thanks mainly to its rugged construction and the skill of its pilots. On 20 February 1942 the US Navy's Lt. Cmdr. Edward "Butch" O'Hare single-handedly saved his carrier, USS *Lexington*, by breaking up an attack by nine Japanese bombers and shooting down five of them in six minutes. O'Hare became one of the first American aces and was awarded the Medal of Honor. The Wright Cyclone-engined FM-2 Wildcat, which served with the small escort carriers, had a better rate of climb than the earlier Wildcats and it could compete against the A6M3 Zero and its descendants. Altogether, some 8,000 Wildcats were built from 1939 to 1942.

By mid-April 1942 the Japanese were heading for total domination in the New Guinea–New Britain–Solomon Islands area of the South Pacific. In the Battle of the Coral Sea in May, the first in which opposing ships did not engage each other, the Japanese lost 80 aircraft and the United States 66. At Midway, 3-5 June, Devastator torpedo bombers, which had fared so badly previously, remained aboard the carriers only because there was no time to embark the new Grumman TBF-1 Avengers. Midway was defended by a handful of USMC Avengers, Wildcats, SBD-2 Dauntless dive-bombers and obsolete F2A-3 Buffaloes and SB2U-3 Vindicators, plus a few B-17Es and B-26s. On 3 June 12 Buffaloes and Wildcats intercepted the first strike by 108 Japanese aircraft, shooting down four and damaging a few others before the Zeros shot down 24 of the US fighters. Six Avengers and four B-26B Marauders launched torpedoes against the Japanese carriers but seven aircraft were shot down and three badly damaged. Despite their disastrous debut the Avenger was destined to become the standard torpedo bomber aboard American carriers. In all, American aviation units lost 85 out of 195 aircraft but Japan's loss of her carriers meant she would never again dictate events in the Pacific.

Deliveries of the F4U-I Corsair began in October 1942 and it was the first US Navy fighter to exceed 400mph (644kph) in level flight. Its "hot" performance and re-stricted forward vision on deck resulted in the first F4Us being used on land by the USMC until Britain's Royal Navy proved the Corsair could be flown successfully off carriers. It finally began operating from US carriers in January 1945 when USMC units and VBF fighter-bomber squadrons of the USN joined in battle in the skies over Japanese-held

islands. On 18 April 1945, over Okinawa, Corsairs dropped napalm for the first time. The F4U destroyed 2,140 Japanese aircraft for the loss of only 189 F4Us in aerial combat.

The Grumman F6F Hellcat, which had first flown in pro-totype form on 26 June 1942, made its combat debut on 31 August 1943 when it was flown by VF-9 from USS *Essex* and VF-5 from USS *Yorktown* on strikes against Marcus Island. It was faster in level flight and the dive than the A6M5 Zero. By the end of 1943 approximately 2,500 Hellcats had been de-livered to operational squadrons; eventually, some 12,275 Hellcats were produced. Almost 75% of all the US Navy's air-to-air victories were attributed to the F6F; its kill ratio was 19:1, accounting for 4,947 enemy aircraft destroyed, plus another 209 claimed by land-based units. During the "Great Marianas Turkey Shoot" in the Battle of the Philip-pine Sea, 19/20 June 1944, the Hellcat accounted for most of the 300 Japanese aircraft destroyed. It was the final carrier battle of the Pacific War.

It was thought that a massive invasion force was going to be needed to storm the Japanese home islands and end the war, but in August 1945 the dropping of two atomic bombs by B-29s on Japan forced its final, unconditional surrender. The reign of terror from the skies had ultimately proved decisive. Brig. Gen. Billy Mitchell, who had died in 1936, had been vindicated and in 1946 the US Congress awarded him a posthumous Medal of Honor.

*"B-17 or B-24, which was the better heavy? We endured
a frustrating two months as the AAF played yo-yo with
our bomber allegiance. We received our Pacific gear.
Soon the infamous warriors of Japan would pay for
Pearl Harbor! Pilot 'Whit' Whitlock received new
orders. Our B-24 summarily taken, we were sent for
B-17 training. We cursed the US Army and reviled the
stupid Pentagoners. How we bitched! Finally, our
bombardier said, 'If you don't like it, go home to your
mommies!' We adjusted OK. The '17s proved to be good
ships; didn't have the speed, range or bomb capacity of
the '24s but they were really maneuverable, reliable,
airworthy craft. What the hell, why fight fate? Maybe
we averted disaster by changing bombers."*

The memories of gunner Don Chase are shared by thousands of
other USAAF veterans still alive today. The "Big Friends" they recall
so fondly are the B-17 and B-24 battlewagons they flew on long-
range penetrations of the Reich in a daily assault on the U-boat
pens, industrial cities and the oil and rocket sites of "Fortress
Europa". Meanwhile, in the Pacific, battalions of huge B-29
Superfortresses rained fire-bombs on the sprawling cities and
aviation factories of Japan and bombed strategic targets throughout
the Empire of the "Rising Sun". They flew in tight protective
formations which maximized their defensive firepower, protected
by escort fighters flying top cover where possible. Crews were well
aware of the exceedingly high casualty rates their missions were
suffering from; still, they went back for more
because it was their duty.

B-24 and B-17 race for first place. Chase's B-17 made it safely to Prestwick:
"We learned of our new orders: Leave the '17 and reorientate ourselves
with the B-24. Shafted again! Unflappable, wry-humored Harold Schwab
arrested our mutinous stirrings: 'Navigator, which way is west?' Ricks
pointed. Deadpan and wordless, Schwab picked up his B4 bag and walked
away. 'Hey, where you going, Schwab?' someone asked. 'Home, I'm just not
interested in this war anymore.' Catch-17, 24!"

B-17 Flying Fortress

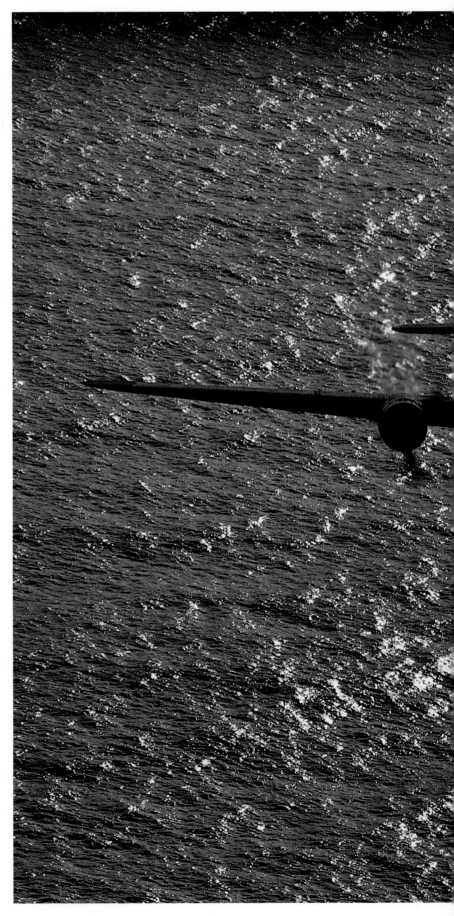

"Up we went into the dark for assembly. The whole 8th Air Force seemed to be up and milling around. My anticipation made the sweating-it-out begin early. Light, when it came, was eerie. A kind of golden light, not strong, not bright, just gold daylight. And then I witnessed something that made man, the bombers, the war, insignificant. It was an apparition bathed in soft, golden light. It was a peek into the unknown. On one side of the sky, in half light, a beautiful full moon set. At my left I saw a beautiful sun rising over the English Channel. Rays of colour fired from the sun. In that light the sun, the moon, and the shoreline were parts of an awesome painting."

The beautiful scene took T/Sgt. Robert T. Marshall, a radio operator-gunner in the 385th BG, away from preparing for battle as his Fortress formation, stacked like three-dimensional chess, headed across the Channel to France. It cloaked the danger from within as pilots struggled manfully to find their squadron, group and wingmates in the inky darkness of another early English morn. B-17s careering through the overcast, off course and at the wrong altitude, gave no warning of collision. Only cold sweat inside a flying suit announced death's unseen and unheralded arrival. Full fuel cells and maximum bomb loads exploded, blowing the silver craft, not yet battle scarred, into a million fragments and a fiery epitaph in the heavens. Ashes of hundreds of crews lay scattered on the waters of the impersonal and freezing Channel and North Sea below.

A B-17 flies low over the Channel's choppy waters. Originally designed in 1934 as a long-range patrol bomber the B-17 was first flown in 1936; more guns were added and it became one of the first strategic bombers, covering the world's oceans from the Atlantic to the Pacific. About 100 B-17Es had been delivered to the USAAC by the time of Pearl Harbor and it equipped a handful of bomb groups who fought the Japanese in the Philippines, East Indies, Guam and Wake. The B-17 operated in the Pacific until 1943.

Naming their aircraft increased crew morale and gave them an identity. Cliff Pyle's (far right, on bomb) B-17F had a peculiar problem of losing power as it gained altitude. Consequently, the crew named their plane "SNAFU" (Situation Normal, All Fouled Up). Cliff recalls, "My crew and I were not too fond of this name and we decided to change the name. 'We The People' was recommended to us by the Gulf Oil Company, whose popular radio program had the same name."

Ben Smith Jr, B-17 radio operator, 303rd BG, says, "There is no man who flew on B-17s who is not sentimental about them. More than any other aircraft, they developed a personality all of their own. The combat crews and the ground crews had intense loyalty to them, born of shared experience. This is shown by the affectionate names they gave them, often that of a wife or sweetheart, and the flamboyant artwork that was lavished on them."

By take-off time tensions were high: "We climbed onto lorries and headed out for the hardstands where the Forts were parked. I can still hear the clanking coughs of the aircraft engines as they struggled manfully in the damp mist and then caught up. We were on board and soon taxi-ing out in trail until we reached the end of the runway. Every 30 seconds a 'Fort' would gun its engines and hurtle down the runway. Finally, it was our time. We always sweated take-off as we were laden with gas and bombs."

Thorpe Abbotts museum, and painted scenes at Horham (top), remain as testament to the "friendly invasion". The "Yanks"' departure was, for Billy Taylor, the end of an adventure: "The atmosphere was ghostly. Daily we visited our old haunts, the control tower, the fire station, where a few weeks earlier we had enjoyed coffee and eggs. All was silent. We hoped we were wrong; they would be back. Alas, it was not to be. But still we visited our beloved Thorpe Abbotts."

A Wright Cyclone with its three Hamilton paddle blades is stationary now but within hours of a mission having been completed ground crews would swarm over the B-17, patching and repairing, getting it ready for the next "big one". Air crews, meanwhile, tried to log a little sack time before "Start Engines". Then the pre-dawn calm of the surrounding countryside would be shattered by the roar of thousands of radial engines being pre-flighted at all points of the compass (far right).

Ben Smith Jr remembers: "The ground crews were extremely attached to their aircraft, even more so than flight crews. A crew chief didn't hesitate to chew out some shave-tail lieutenant for abusing his airplane. B-17s were unbelievably durable and would fly on two engines, or even one. She never let us down. . . . Yes, we loved her. The lady died hard; and when she went down, she went down grudgingly, under protest, and with all her flags flying."

"Texas Raiders" and "Sentimental Journey", above, return to the field. B-17 crews came home time and again with shot-up stabilizers, shredded tires and holed tanks. Sometimes they came through unscathed despite all that the enemy threw at them. Anthony J. Grady, tail gunner with "Ten Batty Boys", 100th BG, recorded in his diary for 4 February 1944: "Really a rough trip. We landed with one bomb bay door down. The pins were broken and it would not come up. We landed with no holes in our plane."

The story of the ground crews is one of devotion to duty. Exposed to the elements, the "paddlefeet's" task was miserable work but maintenance standards remained high. They could do a 30-hour engine change in 8½ hours. Gen. Lewis Lyle, 379th BG, recalled, "A 16-hour day was easy for them. Every day, there was a different fuel load, different bomb load. If their plane came back shot up with dead and wounded aboard, they just cried tears like babies. They loved that airplane."

Bill Rose, pilot, 92nd BG, will always remember the tail gunner reporting formations of B-17s flying into positions behind to protect his rear on the Schweinfurt raid of 14 October 1943: "It was indescribable. This was the first time I had any thoughts that we were in a fight. We thought we weren't going to have the attacks on the tail like we had been getting on our last two missions. Then, all of a sudden, 'Oh my God!' the Germans were letting go air-to-air rockets straight into our group.

"I was fortunate in that one went right past my window. The rocket landed right in the wing of the lead plane, right by a gas tank. I watched it burn and it wasn't long before the entire wing was on fire. The pilot dropped back and the stricken crew bailed out. Eventually, the B-17 blew up. It was a terrible sight to see." At the target Rose looked straight up when the bomb bay doors opened and he could see right into another Flying Fortress's bomb bay:

"If his bombs had fallen out prematurely, they would have fallen on us. Fortunately, I had told my bombardier to tell me one minute before 'bombs away' so I could cut the throttles and drop back to let the lead ship release his bombs right in front of the nose of our plane. When all his bombs had gone and he had closed his bomb bay doors, I pulled up again right underneath him. In my position the German pilots had a real hard time getting at us. The only way they could get to us was to come underneath. I think this was how we were able to survive; protected in every direction apart from underneath. We came home. My crew and I were now 10 nervous wrecks and we didn't sleep much that night. In fact we slept fitfully for about the next year. Nightmares continued most nights until 1945. The battle has affected everyone, myself included, morally and in other ways, for the rest of our lives . . . The nightmare would not, and never will, go away."

At first, German defenses were unprepared for the Fortresses. Maj. Paul W. Tibbets and Col. Fred Armstrong led the first heavy bombing raid, to Lille, on 17 August 1942. Tibbets recalled, "We caught the Germans by surprise. They hadn't expected a daytime attack, so we had clear sailing to the target. Visibility was unlimited and all 12 planes dropped their bombloads. Our aim was reasonably good but you couldn't describe it as pinpoint bombing. We still had a lot to learn.

"AA fire, erratic and spasmodic at first, zeroed in. Three Me 109s moved in for the attack but were quickly driven off by the Spitfires. The only German planes I saw were out of range and I got the impression they were simply looking us over. A feeling of elation took hold of us as we winged back across the Channel. All the tension was gone. We were no longer novices at this terrible game of war. We had braved the enemy in his own skies and were alive to tell about it."

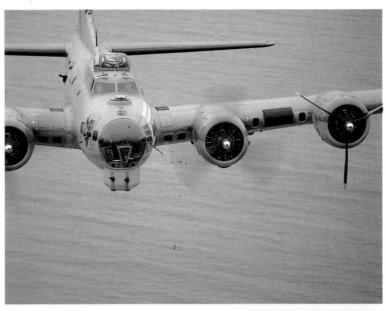

There were no "milk runs" in Italy either. Roy W. Baker, engineer-gunner, 99th BG, had expected one over the Anzio Beachhead: "Everything seemed OK mechanically. We had to feather one engine due to flak on the way to the target area. Of course, the enemy saw we were hurt and the flak was aimed right at us and was so thick you could nearly walk on it. They got No. 3 engine and the prop' ran away so we only had two engines left and we started losing altitude fast.

"We passed near Cisterna at about 14,000ft. They were throwing everything at us by now. The pilot called for me over the intercom and I opened the door to the bomb bay. 'Wham!' A burst of flak blew the catwalk away right in front of me. I looked out of the waist window at No. 4 engine which received a hit and was throwing oil very badly, so to avoid fire we had to feather it. I've flown in '17's that could fly on one engine but 'Mr Lucky' was a log wagon and could not."

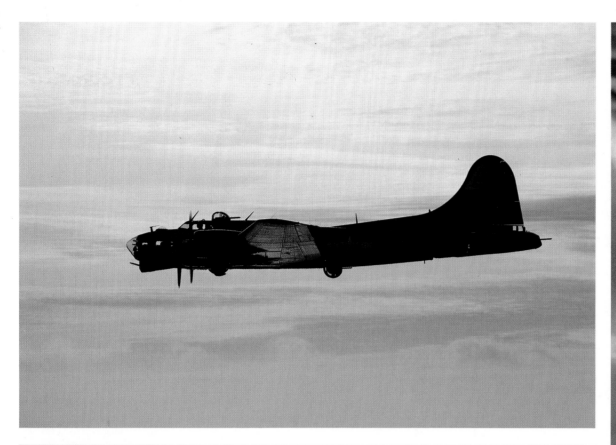

After Pearl Harbor B-17Es of the 11th and 19th bomb groups faced the Pacific might of Japan. Lt. John W. Fields, a pilot in the 435th "Kangaroo" Squadron (Sqn), 19th BG, based in Australia, ran an early mission to Rabaul via New Britain and wrote: "Rotten weather. Couldn't see Rabaul at 14,000ft. Dropped seven 300lb bombs on Buna, a strip we had built and were ready to occupy but the Japs moved in just a day or two before we were going to occupy it and took it from us. We were mad about that."

Horst Handrow, a gunner in the 11th BG at Santo, wrote, "Two Zeros hung over our formation but wouldn't come in to attack. We soon left them behind and headed back to our base. More planes were taking off for Guadalcanal when we landed. We loaded up again with 20 100pounders but no orders came through so we waited. Rain set in that night, and us with planes out. What rotten luck. Death was in the air because the only landing lights we had were trucks parked at the end of the runway.

"We stood there with cold sweat running down our faces. Who wasn't going to make it? We saw a plane light going toward the jungle. 'That isn't the runway', I almost shouted. Too late, with explosion of gas tanks and falling of trees the B-17 went down and started to burn. Five men lost their lives; four got out OK. That was the beginning of our bad luck. We watched out there in the rain until they all landed. We had our fingers crossed."

Tight formations were a must if B-17s were to bring heavy, concentrated fire on enemy fighters. For his actions on 1 May 1943 Maynard "Snuffy" Smith, a ball gunner in the 306th BG, received the Medal of Honor. He wrote, "I hand cranked myself up and crawled out of my ball turret into the ship", then saw, "a sheet of flame coming out of the radio room and another fire in the tail-section . . . I grabbed a fire extinguisher and attacked the fire. The tail gunner had blood all over him.

"He had been hit in the back . . . probably through the left lung . . . another quick burst with the guns and back to the fire . . . to the wounded gunner . . . and back to the radio room with the last of the extinguisher fluid. I found a waterbottle and emptied that on. I was so mad I urinated on the fire and finally beat on it with my hands and feet until my clothing began to smoulder. Our pilot brought the ship in OK and by the time she stopped rolling I had the fires completely out."

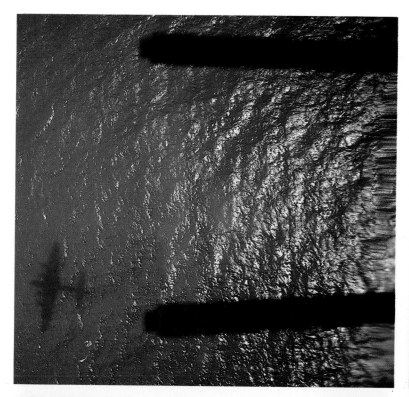

Wilbur Richardson, a ball gunner in the 94th BG: "The ball turret was real lonely, isolated beneath the ship's belly – only 43" in diameter. It got awfully cold: −10° to −70°F. Our Blue Bunny heated suits did not always work efficiently. The fighters came from all directions; the tail as well as the effective nose-on attacks. Attacks were made from 12 o'clock, circled and charged from 6 o'clock level so neither ball nor top turret might get a line on them."

Gunners' claims went into treble figures as kills were duplicated by kindred personnel in other flights, squadrons, and even groups, as they blazed away with their 0.50in calibers in their part of the sky, sometimes endangering their own colleagues in the process. Swastikas and bomb logos on their bomber's nose normally showed these kills and the number of missions flown. "Nine-o-Nine" flew 140 missions in the 91st BG, 8th AF, including 18 to Berlin.

Flying low during an evening sunset this B-17 and B-24 symbolize their wartime partnership. There were arguments about which was the more effective bomber. Jack Houston, a navigator in the 378th BG, felt that, "We B-17 people came along to spread culture among the B-24s. We vizualised ourselves as a sort of Dr. Albert Schweitzer among the natives." The B-24s were cramped and confined. Some thought they could not fly a formation as tightly as the Forts.

Liberator groups derided the Fortress and vice versa. An incestuous relationship ensued between the two crews, and ribald songs of the day, like "I Have No Use for Women", were used to lampoon the bomber:
"A B-17's a fine aircraft
A stratosphere bathtub no less!
It never drops bombs on the target
But ten miles around, what a mess!"

Ben Smith Jr sums up the rivalry: "Originally, the B-17s were called Flying Fortresses. We called them Forts. It was a point of pride to say it. We also called them 'Big Ass Birds'. We were very scornful of the 'Baker Two Dozens', as we derisively called them. It was common knowledge that they could not be belly landed or ditched, and these could be fatal disabilities in the ETO. Of course, B-24 crews reciprocated our scorn. They were as loyal to their aircraft as we were to ours."

Gen. Curtis E. LeMay said of the Fortress: "The Air Force kind of grew up with the B-17. It was as tough an airplane as was ever built. It did everything we asked it to do, and it did it well." Crew did not always think so. One B-17 navigator in England was moved to write, "As for the B-17, I am not ashamed to say that in 1944-45 I regarded her as a slow, flammable old lady who was really out of sorts among fast young friends and who became my potential enemy every time I flew a combat mission."

The tougher missions became, the more some pilots liked it. They had grown callous in the ampitheater of war high above the enemy's lair. Lowell Watts, pilot of "Blitzin' Betsy" in 388th BG, flew one of the toughest, to Regensburg, on 25 February 1944 at the end of "Big Week": "All we had to do was follow the column of smoke down to the earth . . . We turned in for our bombing run. The target was spread out beautifully below us . . . A chance like this was a contact bombardier's dream.

"The bombs went out, we closed our bomb bay doors and turned away from the target. Behind us were three planes, making a bomb run of their own. They looked so vulnerable and all alone back there, but they made the run and pulled in with another formation without losing anyone. Below us our target was rapidly looking like the other one which had been hit by the 15th Air Force before we had arrived. Smoke was pouring upward, rising to about 20,000ft."

"As we go out we have just crossed the French coast. It is only a few minutes now until we reach the target outside Paris", wrote Lt. Olan Hubbard, a group bombardier. His target was the Renault Works, Paris: "I can see the Seine over to our right as it makes its turns and curves. I hope I can follow it all the way because our target lies just in the middle of the second big bend after it enters the suburbs of the city. It looks like a silver snake in the sun's reflection. I already have figured the bombing conditions three times but will do so again. I can't afford to miss today. If I do, I'm sunk. 'OK Bill, turn on the target now . . . back to the left about 5°. OK, we're perfect now' . . . everything's set . . . good grief! . . . the squadron ahead's tearing hell out of the place . . . Boy! I can see their bombs through my sight . . . Check, check, check and recheck. All OK . . . level now . . . level . . . just a few seconds and we can turn . . . here they go . . . camera! . . .'Bombs Away!' "

Abe Dolim (above, far left), a navigator in the 94th BG based at Bury St Edmunds, flew with many bombardiers: "Most usually said 'Let's get the hell of here' after 'Bombs Away', but one fellow I'll never forget said very quietly instead, 'Die you bastards!' Like love, hate is a very personal emotion." He flew 51 missions and refers to his last as a "wingding". In his diary he wrote: "We refused to drop our bombs eight miles short of the target where the rest of the group unloaded. Deputy group lead bombardier was mad as a wet hen because the lead aircraft did not turn the bomb run over to us when they began to experience mechanical difficulties. The whole mess is ridiculous! Nobody seems to give a damn whether we hit the target anymore. What in blazes is tonnage worth if it does not hurt the enemy? Group is sore because we loused up their paper war – I'm glad. To hell with them – tonite I will celebrate by getting plastered and forgetting the whole bloody war."

Coming home on a wing and a prayer and finding a welcome field among the brown brocade of East Anglia is a feeling crewmen like Larry Goldstein, a 388th BG radio operator, experienced: "Over France our navigator was unable to plot a course. I contacted the RAF distress channel for help. God bless them because they answered immediately with a course for England . . . When we broke out of the cloud we were over the Channel. Our landing approach was normal until touchdown . . . no brakes!

"We went off the end of the runway and did a slow ground loop, coming to a halt. Fire trucks rushed to our aid but were not needed. Medics wanted to know if the radio operator was hurt. I was OK! One of the firemen pointed to a tremendous hole in the right side of the radio room. Then I realized we had flown like that for three hours. I was too scared to realize the danger. Nevertheless, it was 25 and home. We walked away from the plane and said our own individual prayers of thanks."

B-24 Liberator

"Fortresses had a larger wing area than the B-24s and were somewhat easier to fly in formation, especially at high-altitude. Straight and level, as on a bomb run, both were good platforms, but in formation there was probably more jockeying of controls and throttles in the B-24s. We often had one pilot on the controls and the other on the throttles for this reason. We overcame the problem to some extent by using the supercharger controls rather than the throttles for such speed adjustments. All this was necessary when the group was flying a tight formation but if the lead ship started evasive action, then we had problems. We were untrained in formation flying at high-altitude until we arrived in England, but with experience the problem was eventually solved after a few months."

Lib' pilots like Bill Cameron faced a tough baptism of fire in the "Big League" in 1942. An equally fierce inauguration awaited B-17 and B-24 crews in every theater of war. Daylight precision bombing midst flak and fighter opposition was not a healthy occupation, even for brave young men. The price of a ticket back to the ZI might be pretty high, but completing a tour of 25 missions in a B-24 and returning Stateside was possible, thanks largely to the rugged construction of the ship. Elmer R. Vogel, a ball gunner in the 307th BG, knew: "Not many airplanes could still fly as the B-24 did with all the damage encountered. She sure took a beating over Balikpapen oil refinery, Borneo, on 3 October 1944, but got us back. With the total cooperation of all on board, and with God's help, we lived to see another day. I guess it just wasn't our time to go."

Each crew christened its own plane with a special name, which seemed to breath life and individuality into that great mass of aluminum, instruments, wiring and driving power; a name which transformed their plane into a warm, vibrant personality. John Steinbeck called it, "The best writing of the war." "All American" was just one of the many hundreds of "personalized" and nicknamed bombers with which the American public have become familiar.

"All American" doubles as a 456th BG Lib'. B-24s based in Libya, and later Italy, bombed oil and rail targets in Romania. Jack Dupont, co-pilot, 456th BG, set out for the Bucharest marshalling yards: "We could not see to bomb. With no fighter escort, we encountered a heavy fighter attack and our plane was badly damaged. We salvoed our bombs and, with two engines out, started across the Adriatic. About halfway we called the crew to prepare to ditch." Far more successful, and memorable, was the classic low-level strike against the Romanian oilfields at Ploesti on 1 August 1943 by 8th and 9th AF B-24s. Bill Cameron, of 44th BG, piloted "Buzzin' Bear" through the inferno: "There were two raging areas of destruction. These were close together with a narrow tunnel of light in between. It seemed that bombers were converging toward that one small area that was free of flame and explosions and then 'Suzy-Q' disappeared in that smoke and we were right behind. I pushed

hard on the control column and headed for the ground. I am sure this near spontaneous action saved our lives. Staring up at us were numerous shirtless AA gunners in gun emplacements with long, black barrels pointing directly at us. We levelled and began a flat turn to the right. I pushed hard on the right rudder but kept our wings from banking with opposite aileron control. It may be that the skidding turn threw the gunners off, but we escaped destruction. Unable to find our

building in the smoke, flame, exploding tanks and the general confusion, our bombs were held too long. I only hope that they fell in an area that contributed to the general destruction. Few aircraft came off target lower than we did. We left the target area pulling about 36in of manifold pressure at 225mph. A year or more later, 18 September 1944, on another low-level mission, to Holland, we had to use about the same power settings to get 170-180mph."

Barrack huts, long derelict and forlorn, were home for American air crews for a year or more. Forrest S. Clark, a gunner in the 44th BG "Flying Eightballs", has vivid memories of his "sack time" at Shipdham (above): "The quarters did receive a ration of coal for the fires but someone was cutting off a piece of the beams in the hut to make firewood! The floor was always wet. The dampness seeped into the beds and the wind across the Norfolk Broads and the Fens rattled against

the huts. The cold was the same damp chill that invades the English cathedrals and in a country without central heating in the 1940s it was most difficult to avoid. Now, when I stand on some old abandoned runway or control tower and look out across an English flying field or old base I hear many sounds – engines warming up, the squeal of landing wheels and the roar of take-offs. However, above all these sounds there are the faint words of a song that comes back with the wind across the

English wheat fields like a whisper from our youth. That song, a favorite of bomber crews, still haunts me and is to me the essence of my combat flying experience. We would be coming back from a mission, tired, disgusted, many times ill from the cold and high-altitude flying. Suddenly, over the intercom, silent on most returns from a mission, we would hear a voice starting with the words, 'Roll me over, roll me over, lay me down and do it again'."

Liberators parade at Lavenham (top) during taxi-ing time like circus elephants, with rudders flapping, brakes squealing and turret guns swishing side to side; the roaring Twin Wasps trumpeting another bitter wartime dawn. Homesick Americans braved the cold of winter and enjoyed the peace and beauty of spring and summer. England's wheatfields and poppy strewn hedgerows gave compensation for the life of combat and work; now, its people, who were their friends, sleep soundly in their beds.

"All American" makes a lo-lo pass over the water. Operating the PB4Y-1 (B-24J) in the South Pacific provided flight crews with the full range of emotions. US Navy PB4Y-1 pilot Paul Stevens remembers, "The excitement, exhilaration, boredom, poor living conditions and, on occasions, stark terror. As a matter of fact, living in tents, sleeping under a mosquito net and existing on dried rations, was enough to make most of the PPCs [Patrol Plane Commanders] downright mean."

A PPC could do just about anything he had the guts to do. Mast-head bombing attacks against Japanese shipping and scoring against enemy aircraft ran up an impressive kill record. Sometimes PB4Ys came up against a convoy. Bombs were fused with a five-second delay and if they had surprise they would make a run against quite large ships. In an attack on Japanese shipping near Baguit Bay, Palawan Island, on 12 November 1944 Stevens was so close to a ship he was "looking up at him!":

"I pulled up and released seven bombs, all of which hit him. A violent skid and I got right back down on the water to mislead the gunners on the escorts. My gunners opened up at point-blank range, hitting the steam line to his whistle because a big plume of steam rose into the air. AA fire hit the bow turret, wounding the gunner and bombardier. All four engines remained running and there appeared to be no fuel leaks. I climbed and got behind some high hills and headed on home."

Oleo legs are extended and the nose wheel doors open as "All American" comes into land. In the cramped confines of a B-24 bombardiers and navigators sometimes sat on the sprung nose wheel doors when not at their instruments. Doors on some models opened inwards, but others, like the ones on this Liberator, opened outwards. Some doors capsized under the weight and the unwary airman was jettisoned into the slipstream, minus his parachute, to a horrible death.

Bombardiers had to put fear of death out of the mind and ignore the fighter attacks and the flak that mushroomed in front. How, when they could see the flash of the AA guns? They could not dodge. They could only sweat it out while they waited for the burst and pray they'd miss. When bombs hit the target, one bombardier at least, "Felt a grand and glorious feeling up and down my spine, and the world looked brighter, even through a gunsight."

On the bomb run lower flying bombers often got in the way of other planes. There were other dangers too. Lt. Ben C. Isgrig, bombardier with 448th BG, had seven bombs hang up on his first mission: "The bottom station failed to release the three bombs in the lower rack and four bombs from above jammed up on top of them. Two of the four were sticking between the wall of the bomb bay and the three bombs in the lower station. It was impossible to salvo them. I was scared to see that the propellers on the fuzes of three of the bombs were turning rapidly, which meant they were probably fuzed and liable to go off at the slightest jolt. I got a gunner to help me and we were able to lift them up one at a time and drop them out. It was a wonder that one or both of us didn't fall out of the bomb bay. It is no joke to stand on a foot-wide catwalk with no parachute at 23,000ft in a 20° below zero breeze and no support, and throw the bombs out one at a time."

In the Pacific long-range B-24s and PB4Ys replaced the B-17 in the island-hopping campaign, and early LB-30 (B-24A) models flew mapping missions to Guadalcanal prior to Marine landings. These were not easy rides. Lt. John W. Fields, 435th "Kangaroo" Sqn, recalls an LB-30 mapping mission on 10 July 1942: "We got No. 4 engine shot out. Zero floatplanes caught us at low-altitude, and we flew 1,000 nautical miles to Moresby with a bomb bay tank half in and half protruding out which we couldn't salvo."

So-called "Snoopers" in the Admiralty Group were equipped with special radar equipment for bombing all surface vessels from low-level and land targets at night, but darkness held as many dangers as the daylight hours. Sgt. Harold Dotterer wrote: "On 11/12 June 1944 our crew bombed Dublontown from 12,000ft. Shot-up by AA fire off Truk Atoll. Two crew were missing when we got out in the life rafts. We were rescued after almost 19 days by a Catalina off New Guinea."

A P-51 approaches the B-24. To Liberator navigator John McClane it is eerily reminiscent of the war: "Fighter pilots were very cautious on how they would approach us, never making a direct approach in case our trigger happy gunner mistook them for the enemy. They would keep out of range of our guns and rock their wings. The P-51 and Me 109 were very similar. I saw one of our fighters shot down by our bomber force because he failed to observe this identification precaution."

The crew of "Little Gramper", 389th BG, are all smiles, but ball gunner Russ D. Hayes (far left) wrote: "Our oxygen masks had built-in microphones that seemed to cause the ice to form around your face, causing frostbite. Goggles were necessary, even in the sheltered part of the ship, to keep our eyelids from freezing shut. Guns were hardly able to fire due to the frost. We had to fire them at short intervals to make sure they would fire when needed."

The ball turret gave excellent coverage and could rotate 360° in the horizontal plane and translate 90° in elevation, but since the gunner was completely enclosed in an aluminum and Plexiglas sphere and totally isolated he probably had the least coveted position in the crew. There was no room within the turret for a parachute pack, so during bail out, with the aircraft probably gyrating, it is small wonder ball gunners ever got out of a stricken B-17 or B-24 alive.

Elmer Vogel, B-24 nose gunner in the 307th BG in the Pacific: "After our third mission the ball gunner, John Warne, asked me if I would like to trade turrets. He did not like the ball. After clearing this with the pilot we decided to fly our fourth mission in each other's turret. I liked the ball better but, since I was 6ft 1in tall and weighing 145lbs, I was really cramped. My knees almost touched my chin but I got used to this. You had quite a view and sometimes you saw too much."

More and more guns were continually added to the Liberator's arsenal to give added protection against fighter attacks. An early innovation was the tunnel gun position (later replaced by the ball turret), but on the low-level strike on the Ploesti oilfields on 1 August 1943, these heavy 0.50in calibers were not needed. Raid veteran Donald V. Chase, radio operator-gunner of "Heaven Can Wait", 44th BG, recalls, "Orders called for a crew of only nine, not the usual 10. The tunnel gun position was to be unmanned because of weight restrictions for the 2,500-mile flight, and because our low-attack altitude and 200mph ground speed would cancel the effectiveness of a single, belly-fired, hand-held .50. The four mid- and rear-section gunners drew straws to determine who would remain. Young waist gunner Ralph Knox drew the *unlucky* straw. He complained and, feeling abandoned, withdrew, not to speak until just before take-off when, woefully, he wished us luck. Ralph was dejected."

Gunners' positions were remote, cramped and difficult to exit from, especially when hit. Sometimes, second navigators used the turret on missions, such as that over Cologne on 14 October 1944 when a 458th BG Liberator flown by Lt. Klusemeyer received a direct hit. Robert Ferrell, the 20-year-old lead navigator, wrote, "The Plexiglas of the Emerson nose turret [top] turns red with blood, the bombardier is blown over from the bombsight back into the nose wheel well, I crank the nose turret to the '0' position, push the bar handle holding the two tiny doors closed down to full open, slip my hands under the second navigator's armpits and pull on him. His head falls back against my right shoulder. I vomit into my oxygen mask and nearly drown from it. I have never seen a human head hit by a shell. I lay him on the strewn floor. With a note of the macabre, I make an entry into my navigation log in the blood lying on my table. The stun of the incident is blown away by the three rings on the bail-out bell . . ."

In the United States B-24 crews flew navigation training missions and men perfected their skills over Arizona's canyons and deserts (above and far right), and California's High Sierras (right); normally excellent weather enabled bombardiers to drop their practice bombs in a "pickle barrel" from several thousand feet. In combat, crews hated the valleys and snow-capped mountain ranges which caused many fatal accidents on bombing missions deep into Germany and northern Italy. Bad weather was the bane of operations for 8th and 15th AF crews in England and the Mediterranean. Pilot Edward R. Glotfelty, 493rd BG, set off for Kempton, east of Munich, which was guarded by 19 guns: "It was a 'milk run', but en route the division encountered a storm front stretching across France with clouds up to 40,000ft and crews tacked on to a 'cluster' of aircraft going to Munich where instead of 19 guns we now had several hundred and they were all firing."

The hazards of flying were, of course, not restricted to combat missions alone. A Liberator was lost over the High Sierras during the war and the route became known as a dangerous one, as a flight engineer experienced for himself: "We were flying over when we hit a 'down draft' and dropped several hundred feet . . . my heavy tool kit got airborne, punctured a hole through the floor and dented the outer skin. We were lucky. The plane to our left flipped over and was flying upside down."

B-29 Superfortress

"The thing was so goddamn enormous that I didn't know how it was going to get off the ground. We thought the B-17 was a big airplane, but this thing was tremendous. I had to get used to the idea that the rest of the crew was way, way back there somewhere. It was a magnificent plane to fly – we went first class. Warm and comfortable. We even had a food warmer. I'm talking about warming up whole dinners. When we were about an hour from the target, we'd plug in the warmer so when we got done with the bomb run and were coming home, we could eat our dinner. It was very important to us that it got plugged in. We were disgusting, I must say. The cockpit in a a B-29 was like an office. There was more than enough room in there and the visibility was incredible with all that glass."

"Little Gem" pilot Robert Ramer's first impression of the Superfort' was certainly awe-inspiring. The huge bomb bay, which could carry eight tons (8,218kg) of M69 incendiaries, was a big asset when, before flying operational missions, B-29 groups in India first had to move food, fuel, bombs and other supplies over the Himalayas to forward bases in China. By summer 1945 all Japan had come to fear the dreaded "Bni-Jus" of XXI Bomber Command (BC) based on Tinian, Guam and Saipan. B-29s made intensive raids on the Japanese mainland, fire-bombing her cities and pounding her aviation and oil centers at will; in February 1945, Robert Ramer wrote: "There is a cloud formation in front of us, a tremendous front. The leader takes the whole goddamn air force right into this cloud bank. Now, we're talking 200 B-29s , wingtip to wingtip!"

Reminiscent of Superfortresses returning to Tinian, Guam and Saipan from raids on Japan, the Confederate Air Force's (CAF) B-29A, "FIFI", is a majestic sight as it approaches for landing in Texas. Some 3,970 B-29 Superfortresses were built, and 528 were lost in combat from April 1944 to August 1945. Their power was incredible – over 105,000tons of incendiaries and over 64,000tons of high explosive were dropped on Japanese targets between June 1944 and August 1945.

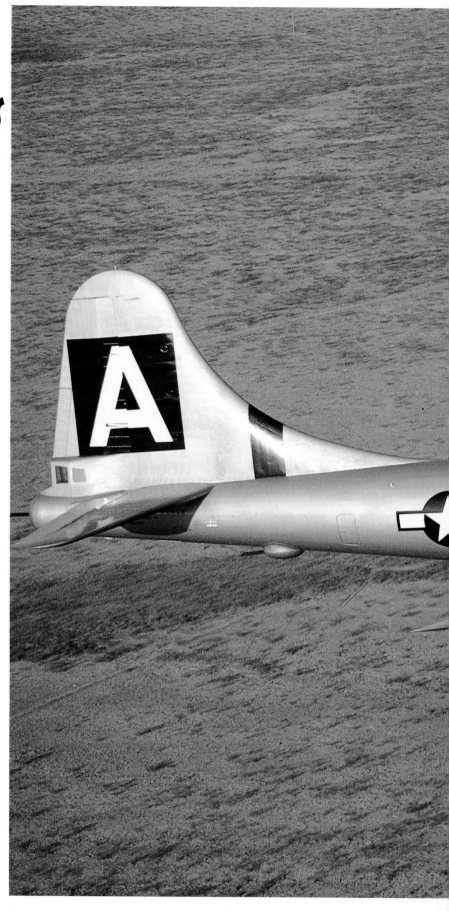

"FIFI" taxies in after flight, the structural "belly" clearly visible. High-level daylight raids on Japanese targets were not productive; losses were becoming prohibitive. Then, in March 1945, Maj. Gen. Curtis E. LeMay employed tactics he had used successfully with the 8th AF in England and put his most experienced radar operators in XXI BC's lead planes, using them as pathfinders designated to mark the target area for bombing with incendiaries in order to burn up large areas of Japanese cities.

LeMay wrote of the first B-29 low-level incendiary attack on Tokyo, 9/10 March 1945: "It didn't take long before there were small tongues of fire throughout the Tokyo urban area. Quickly these small fires spread and merged into larger fires, which in turn merged into a firestorm of incredible proportions. The firestorm consumed so much oxygen that those who did not die by the flames simply suffocated. Huge updrafts from the fire tossed the Superforts like embers over a campfire."

The fires silhouetted the giant B-29s; aboard one was Robert Ramer, looking down into the inferno: "The whole world was on fire. Fires were illuminating clouds at 30,000ft. The plane was actually picked up and thrown hundreds of feet in the air and then dropped again by wind currents caused by the heat of the fires. When we opened the bomb doors, we could smell the buildings and flesh burning. It was sickening. When we got back it was pure exhilaration."

A B-29 packed a Bell tail turret (left) and four General Electric twin 0.50in turrets (above). Gen. LeMay: "In the daylight runs fighters would bother us occasionally – diving into the formation or trying to ram the B-29s, but we'd bother them back. Our gunners shot down a hell of a lot. We positioned our escorts out in front and made them stay there. This forced the Japanese to attack from the rear where the compensating gunsights of the B-29s would handle them. It didn't make the Japanese very happy."

Despite an effective blockade and relentless bombing by an ever increasing number of B-29s – by April 1945 four wings and up to 700 Superfortresses were operational – Japan refused to surrender. Top secret preparations were put into action for specially modified 393rd Sqn, 509th Composite Group B-29s to carry incredibly destructive 9,700lb (4,400kg) atomic bombs to Japanese cities. Commanding Officer Col. Paul Tibbets (above, top left), pilot of "Enola Gay", delivered the first one on 6 August that year.

Yank magazine stated: "The navigator was Capt. Red (Dutch) Van Kirk [with pipe], a young Pennsylvanian with a crew haircut that gave him a collegiate look. Van Kirk was a good friend of Maj. Tom Ferebee, the bombardier [back, third from right]. They had flown together in North Africa and England, usually as navigator and bombardier for Col. Tibbets. They were in on most of the colonel's firsts, and he had brought them into his atomic unit as soon as he was put in command."

Tibbets was to recall, "Ferebee, Van Kirk, and I were working as a team, as we had many times before over Europe and North Africa. As we approached the city, we strained our eyes to find the designated aiming point . . . My teeth told me, more emphatically than my eyes, of the Hiroshima explosion. At the moment of the blast, there was a tingling sensation in my mouth and the very definite taste of lead upon my tongue. This, I was told later by scientists, was the result of electrolysis – an interaction between the fillings in my teeth and the radioactive forces that were loosed by the bomb . . ." Capt. Robert A. Lewis, co-pilot of "Enola Gay", looked across at Tibbets: "The Old Bull's eyes looked awful tired. He looked like the past 10 months, at Wendover and Washington and New Mexico and overseas, had come up and hit him all at once. I says to him, 'Bull, after such a beautiful job, you better make a beautiful landing.' And he did."

Smoke puffs from tires on the B-29's tricycle landing gear: back to base safely. George Caron, tail gunner of "Enola Gay", went on the interphone to Tibbets after the drop: "Colonel, that was worth the 25-cent ride on the cyclone at Coney Island!" Tibbets joked that he'd collect it on landing, but was told, "You'll have to wait 'till pay day." Paul Tibbets had landed "Enola Gay" back on Tinian to world acclaim. On 7 August, navigator John McClane, at Albany, Georgia, for pilot training after a tour of missions in

B-24s, wrote: "The newspapers were full of the story but of course none of them had even the slightest idea what an atom bomb was. The famous mushroom cloud photograph, along with the explanation that the equivalent of 20,000 tons of TNT had exploded over the city, gave us some idea of the destructive power of this new weapon. Weeks later, when pictures of the devastation were released, then and only then, did it sink in that warfare would never be the same again."

A second atomic device, the only other one in existence, was carried on 9 August in the B-29 "Bockscar", piloted by Charles W. Sweeney. He was to recall: "The navigator made landfall perfectly. We passed over the primary target but for some reason it was obscured by smoke. There was no flak. We took another run, almost from the Initial Point. Again smoke hid the target. 'Look harder', I said to the bombardier, but it was no use. Then I asked Cmdr. Frederick Ashworth (Naval advisor to the project) to come up for a little conference. We took a third run with no success. I had another conference with the commander. We had now been 50 minutes over the target and might have to drop our bomb in the ocean. Our gas was getting low. We decided to head to Nagasaki, the secondary target. There we made 90% of our run by radar. Only for the last few seconds was the target clear." Japan cried, "Haisen da!" (we've lost the war) and it was virtually at an end.

Little Friends

"Throughout the years, several impressions of flight and combat remain as strong as ever. The take-off was always my favorite part of flying – the anticipation of being airborne from 'up front', the rubber-streaked concrete runway rushing past faster and faster, the slight bump or two and then the smooth tilting sway of the big metal bird as she strained heavily to gain her element. There was the exhilaration of bursting through the overcast into a bright sunlit sky at 12,000ft just before going on oxygen. On one mission over Holland as far as the eye could see there were American bombers, hundreds of them, surrounded by 'Little Friends' and I was as awe-struck as a youngster at his first parade."

The fighter escorts accompanied the bomber formations from the time they reached the continent until they got back. Many were P-51 Mustangs flying with external wing tanks which they would drop the moment "Bandits" (Luftwaffe planes) were reported entering the fray. The cry "Little Friends coming into the battle area!" was always welcome news to hard-pressed formations of heavies; Eino Alve, a pilot with 453rd BG, was one who was glad of their support. Crippled and flying alone, he was a sitting duck for German fighter planes: "A fighter did pick us up but, thank God, it was a P-47. He came within eyeball range and called over the radio, 'Hello Big Friend, this is your Little Friend. How much fuel do you have?' We were saved. We could have headed for Sweden but with the P-47 at our side we were confident that 'Big Friend' would return us safely back to 'Old Buck', even though two engines were inoperative. In the distance, I could see a sight that never looked better to those weary eyes – the White Cliffs of Dover. We were home!"

P-51 Mustangs close in on the heavies, always a sight to cheer the bomber crews. Robert L. Miller, pilot of "Son Of A Blitz", 863rd Sqn, 493rd BG, went on deep-penetration missions to Germany and as far afield as Czechoslovakia: "Our P-51 escort was cruising up and down the bomber stream when the alert 'Red Bandits in the area!' was given. Our whole crew really perked up. I called for help with, 'Little Friend, Little Friend, this is Big Friend.' He'd respond in short order off our right wing."

P-38 Lightning

"I start firing as the plane is completing its turn in my direction. Tracers and the 20s find their mark, a hail of shells directly on the target. He straightens out and flies directly toward me. I hold the trigger down and my sight on his engine as we approach head-on. My tracers and my 20s spatter on his plane. We are close – too close – hurtling at each other at more than 500mph. I pull back on the controls. His plane suddenly zooms upward with extraordinary sharpness. Will we hit? His plane, before a slender toy in my sight, looms huge in size. A second passes – two – three – I can see the finning on his engine cylinders. There is a rough jolt of air as he shoots past behind me. My eyes sweep the sky. There are only P-38s and the plane I have just shot down."

This diary entry by Charles A. Lindbergh records his shooting down of a "Sonia" over New Guinea during an escort mission for the bombers on 28 July 1944 when the famous aviator was attached to the 475th FG at Hollandia in order to find ways of extending the P-38 Lightning's range. The P-38's great radius of action made it an excellent escort fighter in both the Pacific and Europe. Although slightly slower and less maneuverable than most single-engined fighters, the Lightning could take a great deal of punishment, lose one engine, and still get its pilot home. Japanese pilots respected the P-38's devastating firepower and excellent rate of climb, while the Germans nicknamed it the 'fork-tailed devil'.

The P-38 helped form the backbone of the American fighter force from 1942 to 1945. Maybe not as effective as the P-47 and P-51, pilots like Arthur Artig still wanted to fly it: "I went through twin-engine school, and before I graduated they asked me which plane I would like to fly. They actually acted like you had a choice. I asked for a P-38. They said I couldn't have it because it was a fighter. I said, 'Doesn't it have two engines?' They said that wasn't the point, it was a fighter."

This P-38 blends with the overcast sky as it banks to port. Increased fuel capacities had added in 1943 to their normal long range. Maj. Gen. Bill Kepner, VIII Fighter Command (FC), stated that they could thus, "Go to the bombers' targets and provide protection there during the most crucial moments of bombing. Still, there were gaps in the escort. There were not enough P-38s to cover the bombers from the point where the Thunderbolts had finally to leave them and return and still cover the target area too . . ."

It was such "fighter gaps" that dogged missions throughout the war, creating danger for the bombers despite every effort of escorting fighters to assist as much as possible. Ralph Reese was a B-17 waist gunner on "Smoky Liz". He recalled a mission to Rostock Junkers airplane factory in April 1944: "Our escorts were P-47s and P-38s but they were not around when we were attacked by enemy fighters. We saw eight Fortresses go down and a possible three enemy fighters shot down."

The sight that impressed bomber crewmen like John McClane most was when a flight of P-38 twin-tailed fighters would show up to escort them: "They were usually off at a far distance and at a higher altitude. The contrails showed us the path of the planes as they maneuvered in violent arcs thru the sky. The effect of this sight would send our internal communication system in high pitch of approval and gratitude by all the crew. The P-38s were no better than the P-47s, and maybe not as effective, but it was still a beautiful sight to see our fighter escort catch up with us as we winged our way into enemy territory, or pick us up on the way out. Sometimes on the way out, and other times on the way back, we would fly directly over the White Cliffs of Dover. They were really and truly white, and the sight is breathtaking in their magnificent beauty. They drop straight into the English Channel where the Straits of Dover separate England and France."

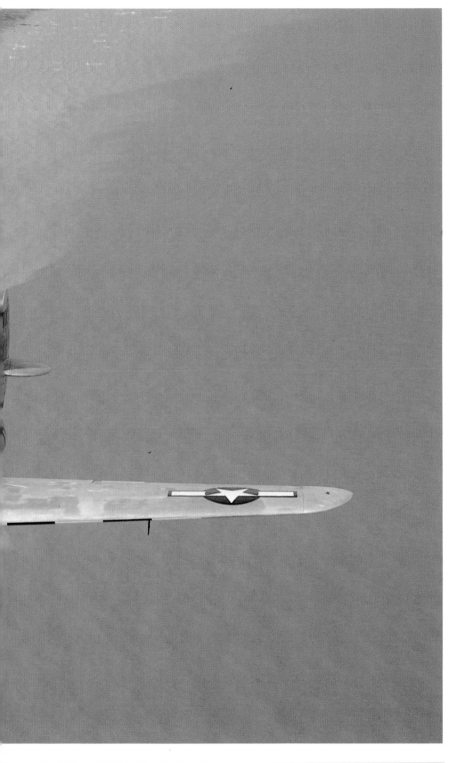

"Buzz jobs", like this one by a P-38 pilot at Lavenham, were a favorite form of recreation for fighter jocks. Photo-recce (PR) P-38s flew low over targets and photographed them before and after each bombing raid. Elliott Roosevelt, of 325th PR Wing, wrote, "Over Europe we had to contend with the new German rocket interceptors that had a tremendous speed advantage over our reconnaissance planes. We photographed targets on flights to and from the Soviet Union, Italy and England."

The Fighter Collection's P-38 – one of only six flyable examples in the world – is painted to represent "Happy Jack's Go Buggy", which was flown by Jack Ilfrey, the first American ace on a P-38. Ilfrey recalled the Lightning as, "A wonderful ship. It went a long, rugged way to winning the war." In July 1942 he was a pilot in the famous "Hat-in-the-Ring" 94th Fighter Sqn (FS) in the 1st FG; what he refers to as, "The experiment, the guinea pigs, the real beginning of the Eighth Fighter Command."

En-route to England they tussled with a Focke Wulf: "July 15, 1942 – I was taking a nap in my Nissen hut when the report went out that a German Focke Wulf Condor was over Iceland. Lightning struck the airdrome and before anybody could think twice, Maj. Weltman was in his P-38, tearing over the airdrome and charging the German's four-motored long-range bomber with his guns. The Germans matched Weltman for quickness. When Weltman closed in, the Nazi gunners made direct hits on the

Lightning's armament assembly, making the four guns on his P-38 useless. Then one of the plane's engines stopped and Weltman made for the airdrome, knowing he was fighting a hopeless battle. By now another P-38, piloted by Elza Shahan, and a P-40 were in the air and getting into position to attack the German plane. Shahan made a pass at the enemy bomber and with the P-40 closing in they knocked out the Focke Wulf" inboard engine. Action came fast. Shahan went into a chandelle, returned to position, and came in close for a side shot, instead of a direct shot. He was within less than 100yds of the German bomber when he pressed the button and let go . . . the four streams of 0.50in caliber tracer, incendiary and armor piercing bullets spelled the end of the Focke Wulf . . . the German blew up so quickly that all he could do was go through the thick debris that was flying in the air . . . Shahan was the first American air force pilot in the ETO to knock out a German plane. For that he got the Silver Star."

The P-38 in the Pacific theater was the scourge of the Japanese. The two leading American aces, Maj. Richard Bong (40 kills) and Maj. Tom McGuire (38), flew it. "Bong, Neel Kearby, and Lynch were the big three in the southwest Pacific as February 1944 began," Gen. George Kenney recalled. "Lt. Col. Tommy Lynch had led the P-38s in their first flight over Dobodura in December 1942. Tommy had led the pack with 16 victories but now he needed four to catch Kearby and five to tie Bong . . .

"On 12 April 1944 we again raided Hollandia with 188 bombers and 67 fighters. Twenty Jap fighters intercepted. Our P-38s shot down eight and listed another as probable. Two of the Nip planes that were definitely destroyed in combat were added to the score of Richard I. Bong, making his score 27, one more than the record set by Eddie Rickenbacker in WWI. The one listed as probable was also one of Bong's victims. He told me the 'probable' had gone into the water in Tannemerah Bay.

"When we captured the Hollandia area, a couple of weeks later, I got a diver to go down where Dick had said the airplane went in. The diver located it almost instantly and we pulled it up. It was an 'Oscar'. The left wing had 11 bullet holes in it, the pilot had been hit in the head and neck, two cylinders were knocked out, and there was no sign of fire. I put out an order giving Bong official credit for the victory – his 28th. The race for aces was over, at least for the time being."

P-40 Warhawk

"Each type of plane has its own strength and weakness. The pilot who can turn his advantages against the enemy's weakness will win every time. You can count on a higher top speed, faster dive, and superior firepower. The Jap fighters have a faster rate of climb, higher ceiling, and better maneuverability. They can turn on a dime and climb almost straight up. If they can get you into a turning combat, they are deadly.
Use your speed and diving power to make a pass, shoot, and break away. You have the edge in that kind of combat. All your advantages are brought to bear on the Japanese deficiencies. Close your range, fire, and dive away. Never stay within range of the Jap's defensive firepower any longer than you need to deliver an accurate burst."

These were the tactics Maj. Gen. Claire Lee Chennault devised for his inexperienced American Volunteer Group (AVG) pilots in China. Ensign Edward Rector, pilot, confirms that the lesson was truly drummed in. He wrote, "Chennault taught us how to utilize the attributes of the P-40 against the Japanese aircraft. The Zero could out-turn the P-40. Every fighter pilot, from the First World War on, has been taught that if you're in a fight, and you have to do a lot of turning, the plane that has the best turn rate can always get on the tail of the other guy. Chennault took that fact, drew on his great knowledge of aerobatic flying, and came up with his thesis.

You might not outrun a Zero in a P-40, but you had him outgunned. Chennault told us to never hesitate to engage in a head-on pass because we had two 0.50in caliber machine guns firing through the prop and four 0.30in caliber guns, two guns in each wing."

Pilots like Rector knew the P-40 was faster than the Zero. "If a Zero turned with you," continued Rector, "you didn't try to turn with him. We'd stick the nose down 10°, 20°, 40°, whatever was required to get out of his way.

The in-line, liquid-cooled engine in the P-40 gave the airplane less resistance than the Jap with his radial engine . . . and once you pulled away from him, you'd climb back up and join the fight again. The Zero and other Jap fighters couldn't keep up with us."

AVG pilots (above) run to their P-40s in China. Chennault never knew how the term "Flying Tigers" was derived from the shark-nosed P-40s: "We were surprised to find ourselves billed under that name. It was not until just before the AVG disbanded that we had any kind of group insignia. At the request of China Defense Supplies in Washington, Roy Williams of the Walt Disney Organization designed our insignia consisting of a winged tiger flying through a large 'V for Victory'."

The shark's teeth design, which added to the AVG's mystique, was less original, as Edward Rector explained: "Somebody had seen a picture of an RAF plane that was fighting in the African Desert that had a shark's mouth painted on it. Being innovative types, some of our guys cut out some stencils and put a shark's mouth on one of our planes. It looked so good they painted every one of them and by the time we went into combat, every P-40 we had was painted that way."

Few P-40s remain today, this one in AVG markings being a rare surviving example. The Warhawk quickly caught the imagination of the American public and media alike. In October 1943 *Flying Magazine* stated, "One fighter pilot in China, crossing the southeastern tip of Hong Kong, saw an airplane silhouetted against the sunset. Without thinking whether the silhouette was that of a friendly plane, a shadow or a bird, the pilot moved to attack. An instant before the six 0.50s would have blazed from his P-40, the other plane wigwagged its wing. A Texas drawl came through the earphones: 'If that's a P-40 in front of me, waggle your wing.' The first pilot waggled in a hurry. These two American planes were the last in the air over Victoria Harbour. With no hesitation, both pilots were attacking. 'Attack, attack, attack' – that is the absolute rule of AAF fighters, the reason they are clearing the Axis from the skies in all theaters of war."

Chinese Nationalist Air Force markings, like those on this Warhawk in 3rd Sqn ("Hell's Angels") livery, were replaced with "star and bars" when the AVG became the 23rd FG and was absorbed into the USAAF. Bob Scott (author of *God Is My Co-Pilot*) became its new commander. Chennault had been his wily tutor – a cunning old fox laying a trap for the unsuspecting Zeros for Scott to spring: "I wanted to go down and get it over with. Over my shoulder I looked at my formation and wondered why Chennault didn't give the word. We were so outnumbered that it didn't matter when we went. 'Oh, General Chennault, call me down. I'm ready. We're ready. As ready as we'll ever be!' The sky above our field was filled with circling, diving, strafing enemy fighters, although some of them stayed up high to form 'top cover' for the strafers. When the fake P-40s were blazing and it was apparent to the Japs that they had caught the green Yankees on the ground with

their pants down, even the top cover couldn't resist. They, too, came down . . . Finally, the decoys were nothing but ashes . . . Then the word we'd been waiting for came, tersely, dramatically: 'Take 'em Tigers, take 'em! They're ripe and waiting. Take 'em Scotty!' Down we went. No verbal orders, just a flip of the rudder and a dipping of my wing for direction. In a flash we were closing in on them. All the Zeros were pulled into tight formation by their leaders, and they were practically parading over the city of Kweilin . . . They didn't see us until it was too late. Twenty or more of them were already going down, and those we didn't burn on the pass broke and ran in all directions . . . I followed one all the way to Canton, 200 miles southeast, and shot it down . . . That day we shot down 34 Jap planes in the victory, but more than that, we became blooded combat men . . . And could I have heard the lament of Tokyo Rose that night it would have done me good . . ."

P-47 Thunderbolt

"The monster stood in all its glory, smelling of oil, gasoline, and, in the cockpit, cigars. It basically overwhelmed me. The engine, an 18-cylinder brute, took up most of the frontal section and, when started, vibrated like it was going to destroy itself. After the engine reached operating levels it smoothed out a bit. The giant engine roars into life as the throttle is advanced and it felt like an equally giant hand grabs from the rear and thrusts the ship forward. Overcoming torque is first line of defense against this monster having its own way. Tail up and then lift-off. A piece of cake flying this machine now its airborne. It takes guts to dive several thousand feet and pull out. You think its curtains. No way can you get her level, but with trim helping she does finally obey."

This 56th FG pilot's description of the mighty "Jug" certainly fits. P-47s were built in the greatest quantity of any fighter in American history, some 15,683 in total. P-47 fighter-bomber groups equipped a total of 31 groups in all theaters by the end of 1944, though only one 8th AF group, the 56th FG, still used the P-47 in 1945. Zemke's "Wolfpack" achieved the highest score of all 8th AF groups, shooting down 674 fighters in the air and strafing 311 on the ground. Two of its pilots, Francis "Gabby" Gabreski and Robert Johnson, each scored 28 air victories to top the American aces in England table. In the Pacific the 318th FG, equipped with long-range P-47Ns with even more powerful engines designed originally to overhaul V1 flying bombs in Europe, destroyed 34 Japanese aircraft without loss on 25 May 1944.

"Big Ass Bird" was a term normally reserved for the B-17 but the P-47 was a real "street fighter" and had many more nicknames, most of them derogatory. The "Repulsive Scatterbolt", "Thundermug", or "Thunderjug" were just a few sobriquets. Although it was the heaviest single-engined fighter used in combat, if an enemy made the mistake of crossing the "Jug's" path while it fired the eight wing guns it was "goodbye enemy". Its formidable firepower was totally destructive.

P-47s and P-51s escorted the heavies over the Reich. P-47s first accompanied the heavies to Antwerp on 4 May 1943. Col. Arman "Pete" Peterson, commanding 78th FG, announced on intercom, "I am making a 90° turn and going down. They're Huns lads! Give them hell! Here we go! Tallyho! OK, stay in pairs now." They were the last words he spoke. By 28 July 200-gallon (757l) ferry tanks below the center fuselage were being carried for the first time and the P-47's value as a long-range escort was proved when two 150-gallon (568l) drop tanks were fitted below the wings to enable it to fly all the way to the target. En route to Berlin on 6 March 1944, Lowell Watts, pilot with 388th BG, was relieved when: "Two silvery streaks flashed past. They were '47s; our fighter escort had caught up with us. The Jerries dropped away, making only sporadic passes. The rest of the way in we had good fighting cover. Violent dogfights flared up, forcing several of our fighters to drop their tanks and head for home."

TFC P-47M is fitted with a bubble canopy, copied from the Hawker Tempest to improve cockpit visibility which was impaired on the earlier P-47 "razorback" models, and likes to wear Normandy invasion stripes. P-47D fighter-bombers equipped 13 groups of the 9th AF on D-Day, 6 June 1944, and 14 by VE Day. Eric Doorly, 371st **Fighter**-Bomber Group (F-BG), dropped low-altitude fragmentation bombing on six German destroyers off the coast of France in August 1944: "When they missed, we went down from 15,000ft – down to strafe them at 485mph – and pulled out within 10ft of the water at about 1,000yds range. The Germans put up a solid wall of flak – big green balls. They started hitting the windshield. I missed the bridge, tried to get down again, but there was nothing but a sheet of flak . . . An 11in section of my windshield was shattered, the left side was out, and the machine guns were just lying there. But I got an explosion out of the destroyer. The whole action took only a minute."

The P-47 landing on a paved runway, but in 1944-45 P-47s operated from improvised strips on the continent and atolls in the Pacific. Lt. Edwards Park's outfit was operating out of a steel-matting airstrip and cluster of tents called Nadzab, on New Guinea, when they got their first P-47s: "It was kind of fun to fly a tail dragger again because you really try to kiss it on when you're landing. It was also a big, comfortable plane with lots of room in the cockpit . . . We loved the bubble P-47s. They were really great planes. All of the olive drab paint was gone and everything was shiny aluminum. And they were fast!" Pilots sometimes had to fly for nine hours or more, only to return to face reporters. P-47 ace Capt. Charles P. London, of 78th FG, told *Air Force*: "I still don't know where they came from. The thing that saved us was our system of sending down one flight after the other – for assurance . . . The Germans scattered like a school of minnows when you toss a rock into the water."

"Big Ass Bird" on a modern patrol – perfectly peaceful. If there was one single thing which summed up the P-47 many would opt for its dive. Lt. Col. James J. Stone, said: "Diving away is the ace in the hole for a fighter pilot. Once, the Focke Wulf could break combat and get away in a high-speed dive. But the P-47 can outdive the Focke Wulf and, since it is extremely well built, will hold together while catching him. What's more, a one-second burst from those eight 50s will down any fighter made."

A different time and place, and more dangerous patrolling. This P-47D "razorback" carries a bombload and drop tank as it climbs near Mont St. Michel, along the northern coast of France, in August 1944. By then the Germans were fully aware of the P-47's abilities; according to Lt. Col. James J. Stone, "Our '47s have been in combat since April 1943. Since that time we've made a believer out of many a German pilot. We worry them and that alone is a big part of our job."

P-51 Mustang

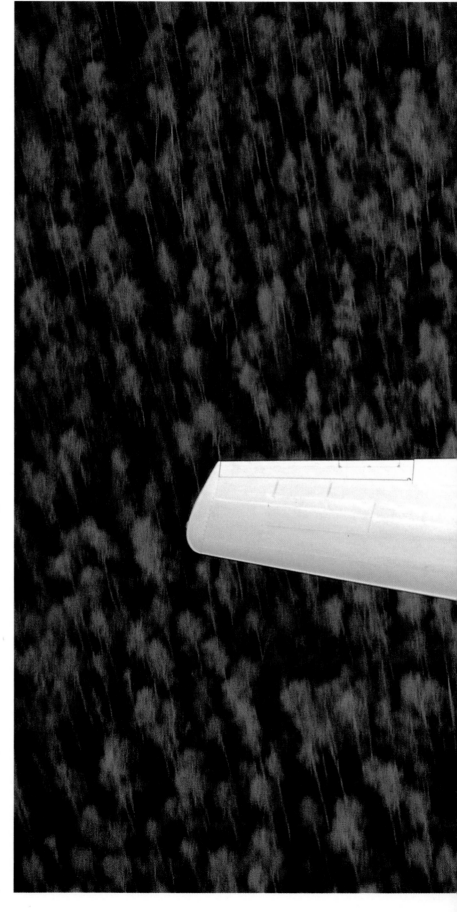

"My first meeting with the Mustang was March 1944. The P-51B could do everything a Spitfire could (except climb) and better, by far the most honest airplane, no bad flying habits . . . Going to Berlin and back in a P-51 was not the most comfortable way to spend one's day, but doing it in a P-51 at least overpowered the discomfort. The P-51D answered all of a fighter pilot's dreams, a wonderful flying machine, a view of the world around, a fantastic gun platform and an airplane designed to combat all enemies, at any distance from base, and with a well trained pilot aboard, a match for any and all comers. My only complaint was that we did not get P-51s a year sooner. Even Hermann Goering knew he was licked when he saw B-17s escorted by P-51s over Berlin."

Capt. Pete Hardiman, 354th FS, 355th FG, recalling the Mustang with some fondness. In November 1943 the P-51B Mustang had been introduced in the ETO. Built originally for the RAF after North American had succeeded in delivering a prototype in just 117 days, the first production Allison-engined model had made its first flight on 1 May 1941. The much faster Merlin-engined P-51, with a range of 2,080miles (3,347km), achieved by the use of wing drop tanks, was far in excess of that available in other fighters of the day. The P-51 was, however, first employed in three groups of the 9th AF as a tactical fighter despite a desperate need by 8th AF's VIII Fighter Command (FC) for a long-range escort.

In March 1944 the red crested Eagles of the 4th FG were first to duel with the Luftwaffe over Berlin when P-51Bs flew to "Big B" and back for the first time. To bomber crewmen like Robert J. Shoens, pilot in the "Bloody Hundreth" which dropped the first American bombs on the German capital, "The very thought of making a raid on Berlin was almost terrifying. The one thing that was going to make it feasible was the arrival of the Mustang in greater and greater numbers."

P-51Bs in colors of the 4th FG in stacked formation, including Chuck Yeager's "Glamorous Glen III", in the yellow-red check nose of 357th FG, and blue-nosed "Old Boy". The first P-51Bs were assigned to IX FC whose 354th FG flew their first mission, a fighter sweep over Belgium, on 1 December 1943. Three days later, attached to VIII FC, they made the first escort mission for the bombers. First in the 8th AF to receive the P-51B was the 357th FG, which flew their first escort mission on 11 February 1944. Many fighter pilots formed partnerships; at its simplest this involved wingmen riding shotgun and keeping "bogeys" off their leader's tail, but others became famous for "feeding" enemy fighters to one another, and in 4th FG's case this was the Don Gentile-John Godfrey combination. Ace and wingman came together on the escort to Berlin on 6 March. Godfrey scored his fifth "kill" to become an ace: "I managed to get on this '109's tail . . . He rolled over and I

really clobbered him. The pilot then baled out . . . Don was going up to another '109. I followed him, giving him cover. He shot this one down and the pilot baled out. We joined up and climbed to 20,000ft again." Two more '109s appeared: " 'You take one on the right and I'll handle the other bastard,' Gentile called over the R/T. We closed in and both opened up at the same time. They both had belly tanks, and the one I fired at blew up. Don's strikes were right in the cockpit and they both

opened up at the same time. At 4 o'clock I noticed one coming in and told Don to break." Gentile and Godfrey took it in turns to fire. Gentile delivered the coup de grâce. Godfrey concludes, "We picked up a lone Fort' about 50miles west of Berlin and escorted it to the English coast. Don and myself were together during all this engagement giving each other cover alternately." The deadly duo returned to the United States in April 1944, finishing as one of the deadliest pairings ever.

Like a pony racing, this Mustang painted in the colors of the 4th FG, guns silent now, shows off its beautiful but deadly lines. Edwards Park recalls that the P-51 was, "Lovely to look at, honest, efficient, hardworking, and dependable. I know men who married their P-51s and are still faithful to them." This is borne out by the number of restored Mustangs, like this one, which proudly carry on the tradition of wartime fighter units such as the famous "Debden Eagles" which claimed the most enemy fighters destroyed. Duane Beeson, one of its most famous sons, stated the most important thing to a fighter pilot was speed: "The faster he's moving, the sooner he will be able to take the bounce and get to the Hun. Never give him an even break. If you have any advantage, keep it and use it. When attacking, plan to overshoot, hold fire until within range, then clobber him down to the last instant. It's sorta like sneaking up behind and hitting him with a baseball bat."

"Glamorous Glen III" of 363rd FS, 357th FG, in formation. The wartime mount of Capt. Chuck Yeager was named after his wife Glennis. The legendary airman is described by his squadron CO, "Bud" Anderson, as, "Aggressive and competitive, but awfully skillful too. In combat he didn't charge blindly into a gaggle of Germans, but with the advantage of having sharp eyes that could see forever, he set up his attack to take them by surprise, when the odds were in his favor."

In a record action on 14 January 1945 the 357th FG claimed 60½ of 161 kills. Maj. John B. England was on the tail of a Bf 109 but out of firing range: "He put his ship in a 90° dive from 32,000ft. At about every 5,000ft he would roll off and do some very violent maneuvers. I did a tight spiral around him. At 8,000ft he made a very tight pull-out and levelled off . . . I made a little tighter pull-out and started firing at 200yds, closing to 50yds. About four feet of the left wing ripped off . . . His ship went into the ground."

On 21 November 1944 Maj. John C. Meyer of 487th FS, 352nd FG, flying "Petie 2nd", finished the day on 15 kills, having destroyed three Focke Wulf 190s in combat. That same day George E. Preddy, CO of 328th FS, 352nd FG, shot down his 23rd enemy fighter. Preddy finished the war close behind Gabby Gabreski's 28 kills. Bomber crews were grateful for the and actions of pilots like these who scanned the skies for the enemy. They were especially pleased on 12 June when a group of about 18 Liberators withdrawing in the vicinity of Rennes were jumped by a dozen Bf 109s, which made a quarter stern attack on them from out of the sun. One of the enemy was about to fire on Ben Isgrig who was hanging in his 'chute after bailing out of his B-24. Preddy intervened and began firing from various ranges and angles: "I got a few hits and [the] enemy aircraft lost most of its speed causing me to overshoot. I pulled above him and was starting another attack when the pilot bailed out at 8,000ft."

"Stick your guns up his coat tails and pull the trigger," Don Gentile said. John Godfrey believed that Gentile had a split-second jump on any other fighter pilot he ever saw: "Your ordinary good flier sees a flock of Huns and counts them. He picks out the one in the rear and dives for his tail. Gentile sees a flock of Huns, and he's after them at the same instant. He'll hit any one he can get to quickest. Reflexes, I guess. When it comes to the pinch, he's got a little something extra."

Bomber crews were also grateful to the fighter pilots. On the mission to Oschersleben on 11 January 1944 Maj. James Howard, 354th FG, single-handedly took on 30 enemy fighters and scattered them, continuing to bluff them away from the bombers even after his guns jammed. Joe Wroblewski, pilot with 351st BG, wrote, "Watching this one fighter escort bolstered our confidence for survival and we all admired his guts to hang in there with us." Howard received the Medal of Honor.

P-51 pilots and their chargers were feted by bomber crews. Ben Smith looked upon the young fliers as, "Medieval knights as they descended from the heavens in their gaudily painted aircraft," but realized that, "The curtain was ringing down on knight-errantry for the last time." A B-29 pilot recalls, "We were the truck drivers and the fighter pilots were the racing car drivers. They didn't have to stay on the road like we did but they were great to have along. Fighter pilots were into weird paint jobs and war stories. All razzle-dazzle." Donald Emerson's P-51 sported Donald Duck; Col. Roy Caviness's (CO, 78th FG) was "Contrary Mary"; while scantily-clad, aerodynamically sleek and sinuous pin-ups, their smooth vibrancy imparted by Elvgren, Petty and Varga's masterful use of the airbrush, inspired crew chiefs like Donald Allen in the 4th FG, who swapped spanners for brushes and fashioned masterpieces using aluminum as their easel.

A P-51 Mustang at silent repose in a setting sun. Mustang escorts were widely used on raids deep into Germany, and over Japan, mainly because of their considerable range achieved by the use of wing drop tanks. In February 1945 P-51Ds flying from Iwo Jima escorted B-29s. On 7 April P-51Ds penetrated Tokyo airspace for the first time. Time and again they rode to the rescue of B-29 pilots like Robert Ramer: "You know the movies when you see the Indians are totally surrounding the little group of pioneers and suddenly there's the music and here comes the cavalry? Those Mustangs, they were our cavalry! One mission especially, we were going to Tokyo and there was cloud cover above us. We knew there were Mustangs above those clouds. The Japanese came up and went right up through the clouds so they could get above us and come down and give us hell. Suddenly it was raining Zeros! They were coming down smoking or had two Mustangs chasing them. Wow!"

Low and Below

"Pulling up to get over the ridges surrounding the targets, we could see columns of dust from the 'dromes. It was apparent that the enemy had not been caught completely off guard. As results proved, three minutes is not enough warning for adequate defense. Several Jap airplanes were taking off and four or five were in the air, low and climbing. We tightened our formation. A 'Sally' broke through our formation in attempting to clear the 'drome, and we gave him a burst. He made no effort to fire or to turn. He went down. Three more Nip planes headed into us. We fired and all three crashed. Another started through us directly in line with my ship. I opened up on him. His right wing exploded, and he dove into the ground. One ship ground-looped trying to take-off... We were extremely low."

Col. Donald P. Hall, describing a raid by mediums on Rabaul airdrome in 1943. Fast twin-engined medium bombers such as the B-25, B-26 and A-26, were introduced in 1940-42 for bombing missions over shorter distances and at lower altitudes than their four-engined brothers-in-arms. B-25 Mitchells never operated from England with American crews but saw extensive action in every other theater of war, predominantly in the southwest Pacific where B-26As and B-25Bs had first gone into action against the Japanese in April 1942; the B-25H actually replaced all B-26 Marauders in a couple of very different roles: attack bomber and night fighter.

B-17 Flying Fortress led by a black A-26 Invader would seem an unlikely pairing but in World War II the 25th BG in East Anglia operated both – the Fortress as a weather reconnaissance ship, and the Invader on spy-dropping sorties over Germany. The pacy, long-ranging A-26C, painted gloss black overall and modified to parachute two secret agents safely, proved ideal for the task of penetrating the German defenses to make successful drops over the environs of Berlin in 1945.

B-25 Mitchell

"We just sighted the outskirts of Kobe. The skies are still vacant, and that scares you a little. We're over the edge of the city, coming in at 2,000ft. Lt. Sessleris says, 'That's our baby.' I see the target. We roar across the city, raising such an almighty racket the noise kind of bounces back, it seems like, and the Japs down there are running back and forth in the streets like so many ants in an ant hill. They don't seem to catch on to the fact that the Stars and Stripes Forever are right up there over their heads, equipped with plenty of horsepower and plenty of bombs and that darned old 20-cent bombsight. 'Let 'er go. Sess,' Smith yells to the bombardier. Sweet as you please. That B-25 takes a sudden uplift, a little bit of a lurch. Hirohito, the Yanks have arrived."

Patriotism was high when Sgt. Edward J. Saylor, a B-25 engineer-gunner, spoke these words to *Yank* magazine following his participation in the raid on Kobe, Japan, on 18 April 1942. The B-25 will forever be remembered as the airplane used by Lt. Col. (later Lt. Gen.) James H. Doolittle's famed "Tokyo Raiders" which made attacks on Tokyo and three other Japanese cities. Named after Brig. Gen. Billy Mitchell, the headstrong but fearless aviator who was court-martialed in 1925 for his outspoken belief in air power, the B-25 excelled in the Pacific, where it replaced the B-26, making daring mast-head and skip-bombing attacks on Japanese shipping. By the end of 1944, 11½ medium bomb groups were equipped with the B-25 overseas, including units in the Mediterranean, CBI and Alaska. When production ceased in 1945, 9,816 B-25s had been built for the USAAF.

B-25J Mitchell, with RAF fin flashes, in flight. The 12th BG flew 57 B-25Cs across the South Atlantic and Africa to Egypt, from where they made the first raid in support of the British forces on 14 August 1942. Three more B-25 groups joined the US 12th AF in North Africa following the invasion during Operation Torch in November 1942; B-25s were then used successfully on anti-U-boat patrols. The B-25J was the most widely used Mitchell and 4,318 were built.

B-25J "Panchito" takes off. The first B-25As were fitted with hand-held machine guns. Combat revealed serious deficiencies so tail and waist guns and windows were replaced on the B-25B with power-operated turrets; two 0.50in guns in a Bendix top turret and two more in a retractable belly turret were added later. The bombardier's hand-held 0.30in caliber nose gun was retained but removed later by "Kenney's Kids" (5th AF) who replaced it with two pairs of twin 0.50in guns, and added two more pairs, in fuselage blisters, for strafing. Even so, they did not become invincible: during the second Battle of the Philippine Sea, 26 December 1944, Paul Stevens, PB4Y-1 pilot, reported, "The B-25s started their attacks at low-level, strafing as they went in. The return fire from the Japanese ships was extremely heavy and several B-25s burst into flames and crashed. One flaming B-25 crashed into the Japanese destroyer. The B-25s were taking a terrific beating and not many were getting through with their attacks."

Smoke pours from the B-25's starboard engine, but it isn't damaged. War correspondent Lee Van Atta recorded the B-25 raid on Simpson Harbor, Rabaul, in November 1943: "B-25s roved in and out of the smoke. As one, Henebry's lead ships opened fire, selecting their bombing targets with the speed so essential to successful attack bombardment. Henebry dove down on a 5,000-ton freighter-transport, dropped a bomb directly down the hatch which we could see explode; Ellis, flying so low his B-25 looked like a speedboat, roared against a 4,000tonner . . . Wilkins' right wing was almost severed in half by a powerful burst from the heavy cruisers. Fighting controls all the way, he engaged a destroyer leader, scoring a direct hit on it that spelled doom for the war vessel. Then, barely retaining his grip on his mortally injured Mitchell, Wilkins raced on to level a waterline hit on a freighter transport. He climbed but then flipped over on his back and crashed into Simpson Harbor."

Another day dawns and a strike on a Japanese task force might conceivably be called were it 50 years ago. Paul Stevens, PB4Y-1 pilot, recalled just such a day: "Pilots were preparing to man their aircraft. I went over to discuss the possibility of a joint attack. Their flight leader had just informed them they were going to launch an attack against this force. This same flight of 12 B-25s had started out earlier for a strike against an airfield in the Manila area. They had sighted this Japanese task force but because of strong opposition, had broken it off. When they were told that they must return for another attack there was much consternation. They realized, as I did, that this was an extremely formidable force, and chances for a successful attack and return were extremely doubtful. I advised their flight leader that I would be making an attack and would like to cooperate with them. He said they were bombed up and were ready to go and had no desire to wait."

Apart from equipping the 13th AF in the South Pacific, the war's most deadly medium bomber also operated with USMC squadrons. It did not just bomb either, almost one-fifth of the B-25Js were completed as or modified to ground-skimming strafer gunships after they entered service, because the great majority of targets in Asia and the Pacific were too tiny to hit at anything more than tree-top height. The picture shows a 7th AF B-25 strafing Japanese positions on Wotje Island in the Marshalls.

B-26 Marauder

"ALEX . . . JOE . . . STEVE . . . ED . . . AND BILL. You know them. Alex, who used to bring your groceries . . . Joe . . . Steve . . . Ed and Bill, who used to go with little Sally Miller. Likeable, quick-to-laugh young Americans. Give them the best aerial schooling in the world, put them in a rocket-fast, Martin B-26 Marauder, and they're a flyin', fightin' team that wins! . . . . the Martin B-26 Marauder. Sleek, graceful, packed with speed, power and punch, it's the kind of plane that makes young America's eyes light up . . . makes him say, 'Put me down for the Air Force!'"

Martin Aircraft's advertisement, October 1943, certainly lauded the attributes of the pacy Baltimore bomber but a spate of training accidents during 1942 earned it an unwelcome reputation as a "flying coffin". Arthur Artig saw two columns of smoke at the end of the runway: "I asked a crew chief what they were, and he told me it was the plane I was going to learn how to fly. Two of them had gone in that morning. I walked down the flight line and looked at those planes and they looked like monsters." Ribald ditties appeared: "Oh, why did I join the Air Corps?/Mother, dear mother, knew best/Now here I lie 'neath the wreckage/Marauder all over my chest." Twice the USAAF considered terminating production but much to the surprise of many the B-26 had, by VE Day, established a record for the lowest loss rate of any American bomber.

B-26A Marauders based in Australia were among the first to see action – in April 1942 – against the Japanese but the B-26 disliked rough, improvised landing strips. Range and weight limitations led to its replacement in the Pacific by the B-25 in 1943. It was tough though; pilot Arthur Artig wrote: "A couple of guys landed the wrong way in a trainer. A B-26 clobbered them and drove their airplane right into the ground. Killed them both, destroyed that airplane and all that '26 had was a dent in the wing."

"'Achtung, feindliche Flugzeuge!' It is probably about 10:30 hours when the Nazi Jagdführer of the Holland fighter defence area is given this warning of enemy aircraft approaching . . . At 11:00 hours Jagdführer Holland learns that the generating station at Ijmuiden . . . has been attacked. By 11:03 the hit-and-run raiders are reported across the coast once more. A minute later they have passed out to sea and are away. Then the bombs, having delayed fuzes, start to explode."

That report in *Target Germany* describes the first B-26 mission in the ETO: to a generating plan at Ijmuiden in Holland on 14 May 1943. Three days later, all 10 attacking B-26s were shot down over the same target. In that spring of 1943 the sleek shaped bombers had begun equipping the 8th AF in England. During the summer Marauders were used in a medium-level bombing role, escorted in tight box formations by large numbers of RAF Spitfires.

In October 1943 B-26 groups were transferred to the 9th AF for tactical missions in the Allied build-up to the invasion of Europe. On D-Day black-and-white striped 9th AF B-26s flew 742 sorties in support of Operation Overlord. Arthur Artig, pilot, says, "A lot of our missions were involved with cutting the Germans off by busting up the bridges and roads." Flak proved the constant scourge of such B-26 operations, as this 386th BG B-26 minus its wing tip graphically demonstrates.

B-26C "Carolyn" sweeps in low, its prominent Pratt & Whitney Twin Wasps to the fore. Enlarged air intakes were added to B-26B models onward so that filters could be fitted, when required, to protect carburetor intakes during desert operations. Omaha-built Marauders ushered in a new era with a wing of much wider span to compensate for the higher wing loading and a new training program for pilots of twin-engined aircraft to put the B-26's ills behind them. Veteran pilots had little trouble with the Marauder's high stalling and landing speeds. A pilot flew his B-26 to Port Moresby for four hours with one engine dead; another flew for a week with a patched bed sheet in place of a hole in the elevator. In August 1943 Col. Lester Maitland, CO of 386th BG, said, "The B-26 in skilled hands is no more dangerous than any other aircraft. Statistically, the B-26 has made a remarkably high record in operations. In combat these airplanes are able to take severe punishment from flak and still get home."

Night photography was one B-26 speciality. Sgt. Temple Lowe was a rear gunner with 25th BG and recalls, "Our mission was to take pictures of V1 sites, marshalling yards and troop movements. We carried 20 100lb magnesium flash bombs which we dropped at the pre-assigned altitude of 12,000ft. We had to fly a perfectly straight course over the target area with the wings level in order to get a good overlap of the pictures. It was just like a bomb run."

A-26 Invader

"Lt. Cmdr. Stephen H. Simpson Jr, US Navy, was my boss on the secret OSS (Office of Strategic Services) missions that we flew in the A-26. It was needed because of its range, bomb bay space and speed for a special mission, low-level at night and at tree-top-level all the way to Berlin. Steve Simpson talked Doolittle people at 'Pinetree' (8th AF HQ) out of two A-26s; or rather convinced them that we needed two A-26s. After headquarters agreed to let us have the planes Steve wanted to go back and try for a third A-26. At RAF Bovingdon we picked up the first A-26. The fact that we didn't even know how to get into the 'plane, and the fact that I had never flown one, didn't faze us. We flew it back to Watton."

Col. Robert "Paddy" Walker of 25th BG, who piloted 21 OSS missions, recalling the audacious circumstances which led to the A-26 being used to drop 28 teams of agents deep into Germany in 1945. The fast and agile low-level attacker and deadly intruder aircraft arrived in the ETO in September 1944 for assignment with the 9th AF. A-26s saw action for the first time on 6 September when 18, attached to the 386th BG as part of a force of 545 bombers, attacked Brest. On 17 and 19 November 1944 Invaders of the 416th BG made bombing attacks from 6,000ft (1,829m) led by glass-nosed Havocs until glass-nosed A-26Cs satisfied the requirement for a light bomber operating at medium-altitude. Though a late-comer, the A-26 overcame a period of uncertainty in 1944, replacing the A-20 in combat units and winning the admiration of the crews who flew it.

Black smoke erupts from a nacelle and the tricycle landing gear strains as 4,000 horses breathe life into the shoulder-winged B-26B "Sugarland Express". The A-26B was the fastest American attack plane of the war with a top speed of 355mph (571kmh), and packing no fewer than 22 guns. For offense, A-26Bs normally carried six nose-mounted guns, four blister guns on the fuselage sides, and eight guns in four optional underwing pods; as well as two top turret and two belly guns for defense.

The A-26C medium bomber variant, like this preserved gloss black example, normally had only six machine guns: two in the nose and two in each turret. Top speed was increased to 370mph (595kmh) and a co-pilot-bombardier was added as a fourth crew member. Carpetbagger A-26C Invaders were also painted gloss black (for operations during the moon period), and had a hand-picked crew consisting of pilot, two navigators (one visual and one on "Loran"), a sergeant (to assist the two agents) and a tail gunner. The A-26C, with its lightning speed, good range and, equally importantly, the bomb bay space for two OSS agents, was ideal for low-level spy-dropping missions, but on practice missions to Holland in January 1945 it revealed that its "hot" performance meant that agents could not be dropped safely: so, early in February, modifications were made to enable the first "Hammer" mission, to within 10 miles (16km) of the city limits of Berlin, to go ahead on 1 March 1945.

Lt. William G. Miskho, the visual navigator on the mission, recalls, "Maj. John 'Nobby' Walsh (the 'Loran' navigator for the mission) and I spent two full weeks on our flight plan. We would have to go over the continent at 500ft and fly a course to avoid all the thousands of barrage balloons that the Germans put up every night. They changed these positions continually. We managed to avoid the balloons and headed for the drop point. Radar was unable to pick up our blip in time to do any damage, although the tail gunner told us that he did have a little gunfire but nothing very close. We had to fly over our original target area. It was flooded within 20 miles. Just soon enough for us to locate our target we slowed our airspeed for the drop, made a target run and dropped the agents in the correct field. We did not realize how successful we really were until after the war. Following the drop we headed straight home and landed with barely enough fuel to park."

Frenchmen also flew black Invaders. Doug Walker, an airborne dispatcher based at Lyon, remembered: "As we approached the airfield, which was used jointly by the American and Free French air forces, an A-26 zoomed directly across our nose and headed down the runway ahead of us! The American colonel in charge told us, 'Those A-26s are flown by Frenchmen who ignore all landing pattern discipline. They'll cut in front of you with complete abandon, with 'C'est la Guerre' attitude'."

Apart from missions at night, Invaders were used in many roles in World War II, including photo-reconnaissance. As early as 1942 it was planned to replace all other mediums with the A-26 but production delays, for which air chiefs were inclined to blame the Douglas Company, kept acceptances to only 21 airplanes by March 1944. Invaders entered the war in the Pacific in January 1945 and led some GIs to remark, "I wish it could have got here sooner."

The last propeller-driven twin-engined bomber to be built for the USAF, Invader production was halted at war's end in 1945 when all outstanding contracts were cancelled and only 2,450 A-26s had been delivered, too few to make an overall impact on the outcome of the war. Gen. "Hap" Arnold had stated that he wanted the Invader, "For use in this war and not for the next." Ironically, the A-26 fought on in Korea and Southeast Asia, thus completing a quarter-century of service.

In July 1948 the USAF abolished the "A" for Attack prefix and all surviving Invaders were re-designated B-26, the former designation of the Marauder. Ironically, 9th AF A-26s had made their group debut flying with three groups of B-26s on 19 November 1944 when 41 Invaders, led by eight A-20K Havocs, bombed the German ordnance depot at Merzig from 6,000ft (1,828m). The wartime photo shows a 9th AF Invader dropping its "eggs" over the Siegfried Line in the winter of 1944-45.

Flying from the Flat Tops

"We landed at Floyd Bennett Field to fly a huge 'FDR' letter formation as Mrs Roosevelt spoke the ceremonial words and swung the champagne. Letter formations are terribly dangerous ... We joined in with all the air groups located up and down the East Coast. There were 1,200 naval aircraft over New York. It was a wild day. The fleet was in, and President Harry Truman was going up and down the Hudson in a destroyer reviewing the ships. It was a sight I'll never forget. Together, we were the Argonauts, Ulysses, Aeneas: we had endured and finished, and home was ours. We made a big circuit of New York and some F4Us got into a tail chase. One after another, they went looping up and down the Hudson, and I think some of them went under the George Washington Bridge."

Gerrit Roelofs, F4U pilot, coming aboard the USS *Roosevelt* on Navy Day, 25 October 1945. Landing on a large flat top like the USS *Roosevelt* was as difficult as landing on a small ship or "jeep carrier" like the USS *Rudyerd Bay*: "They'd bounce up and down like corks. The *Rudyerd Bay* would list heavily when turned into the wind for a pre-dawn raid and you'd be looking down off the side of the deck, right into the ocean. When you taxied up to the catapult, the wheel of the TBF was only a few inches from the coaming. You'd creep forward with the brakes squealing. It was what you had to do, and you just went ahead and did it." Despite their unique difficulties the naval pilots flying from carriers did a first-rate job and without them the war in the Pacific would have been very different..

Fleet fighters like the outstanding Grumman Wildcat flew top cover for the Grumman TBM/TBF Avenger torpedo bomber. Both aircraft joined in the battle at Midway on 3-5 June 1942 when USS *Yorktown*'s complement of 27 new F4F-4s had folding wings, for greater accommodation aboard carriers, and packed six machine guns instead of four. There was no time to embark the new Grumman TBF-1 Avenger but it was destined to become the standard torpedo bomber aboard American carriers.

F4F/FM Wildcat

". . . In the first run I fired into the two trailers in the last vee. I had to pull up to let them fall away . . . I had fired at the starboard engine in each ship and kept shooting each time till they jumped right out of their mountings. This caused both these planes to veer round to the starboard and fall out of the formation . . . I pulled away slightly while the third plane skidded violently and fell away, then went back in . . . still shooting at the engines. The engine fell out of this fourth plane too . . . By this time the Japs, still in formation, were right on top of the release point. They had *to be stopped any way at all: there were five of them still. I came in close, shot into the fifth one till he fell away and then gave the remaining four a general burst until my ammunition was exhausted."*

This encounter by Lt. Edward "Butch" O'Hare occurred on 20 February 1942 off Rabaul when he single-handedly saved his carrier, USS *Lexington*, by breaking up an attack by nine Japanese "Betty" bombers and shooting down five in six minutes. Lt. Cmdr. John S. Thach, innovative skipper of VF-3, observed that, "O'Hare's firing was a real record. We figured that he used only about 60 rounds to each of the planes he knocked down. To knock down five planes with one load of ammunition is something only a fighter pilot can appreciate." O'Hare's action taught Thach and his men a lot: "Those Japs came in with great determination. They never hesitated a second . . . The second nine never faltered and came right on in to the bitter end." Determination, however, was only part of the story; aircraft had to be good performers, soundly constructed and in able hands.

This action by O'Hare showed that the only real defense for a flat top, or any other ship at sea, against air attack, was an aircraft. Although slower than other American fighters and outperformed by the Zero, the Wildcat averaged almost seven enemy aircraft shot down to every one F4F lost. This can be attributed to its rugged construction and the skill of pilots like O'Hare, who became one of the first American aces and was awarded the Medal of Honor for his defense of the "Lady Lex".

Missing from this modern-day survivor is a load of any kind. Underwing bombloads restricted the F4F. Maj. Joe Foss recalled its agility in a dogfight: "Eight of us took off. Soon we jumped eight Zeros and got involved with six of them. We managed to get 'em but lost one of our boys. Then we spotted the destroyers. I decided to go in last and as the boys were peeling off I noticed the float of an enemy plane poke down through the overcast. I swung behind and when he dropped clear I made a pass. I came in fast. I thought I'd run into him and couldn't shoot. As I went by a guy in the back seat with a free gun turned that old baby on me. The line of bullets stitched right up the cowling. I pulled my head back because I thought I was going to get it in the teeth.

One bullet went through the canopy past my left temple. The plane seemed OK so I dived, came up again and got him with a belly shot. Then a second one jumped me and I got him the same way."

Wildcats sported their own distinctive artwork. These famous felines are the "Felix the Cat" insignia (top) of VF-3 and the VC-12 insignia (bottom) painted below the windscreen of an Eastern Aircraft Division FM Wildcat. VF-3's two most famous pilots were Lt. Cmdr. John Thach, famous for the "Thach Weave" fighter maneuver, and Lt. Cmdr. Butch O'Hare. Thach finished the war with six-and-a-half kills; O'Hare was credited with seven before he was killed on 24 November 1943.

Hook down, a Wildcat pilot straightens out from his nose-high turn and comes in for a deck landing. At first, all the pilot could see was a "roger" from the LSO, or landing signal officer, both hands outstretched. When he signalled "cut", the pilot had to chop the throttle, ease back on the stick, coast in two knots above stalling speed, and wait for the big jerk of the arrestor wire to bring his fighter to an abrupt halt on the deck. Hitting a heaving, pitching carrier was never easy.

Cruising above the cloud cover, this head-on angle offers a good view of the Wright Cyclone on this powerful FM-2, the final mark of Wildcat and considered by many to be the most effective. It was built by Eastern Aircraft who built some 40% of the 7,251 Wildcat total. In the thick of the Pacific action throughout the war, based on land and at sea, the little fighter was particularly valuable because of its ability to operate from small carriers.

Smoke bellows from this F4F-3 as it starts up for take-off, a dangerous moment for an aircraft, for to be caught by a raid was almost certainly fatal. Hunter Reinberg flew F4F-3s with the "Flying Leathernecks'" VMF-121 and remembers his first strafing victory at Munda in 1942: "My gaze was transfixed by a Zero rolling rapidly down the taxiway. It never occurred to me to be a sport and let him get airborne . . . The urge to kill overtook me completely. Oh Boy What a Set-up!"

F4U Corsair

"He never changed his course much, but started an ever-so-gentle turn. My Corsair gradually closed the gap between us. 'As long as he is turning, he knows he isn't safe. It looks too easy.' Then I happened to recall something I had experienced in Burma with the Flying Tigers so I violently reversed my course. Sure enough there was his little pal coming along behind. He was just waiting for the sucker, me, to commence my pass on his mate. As I turned into this pal. I made a head-on run with him. Black puffs came slowly from his 20mm cannons. His tracers were dropping way under my Corsair. I could see rips in the bottom of his fuselage as I ducked underneath on my pass by. The little plane nosed down slowly, smoking, and crashed with a splash without burning or flaming."

Maj. Gregory "Pappy" Boyington, who became the leading Marine Corps' ace with 28 victories (including six with the Flying Tigers), describing one of five he destroyed during his first day with VMF-214 (known as the "Black Sheep Squadron") on an escort mission for dive bombers and torpedo bombers attacking Ballale airfield, Bougainville, on 16 September 1943. Boyington and his fellow pilots were gratified to be flying the new and fast inverted-gull winged fighter, the F4U Corsair, after so many missions in the 100mph (161kmh) slower, older, but durable Wildcat. At first, the Corsair had problems operating off aircraft carriers but the "Flying Leathernecks" tamed the hot fighter and used the F4U very effectively from land bases like Henderson Field where F4Us first saw action with the "Cactus Air Force" during the defense of Guadalcanal in February 1943.

Flaps and arrestor hook down, this F4U-7 Corsair simulates a deck landing aboard a flat top. Rex Beisel's design was the first Navy plane built around the Pratt & Whitney 2,000-plus hp Double Wasp. The wing was gulled downwards to give the 13ft 4in (4m) diameter props sufficient ground clearance and to avoid extending the landing gear; the wheels were retracted backwards and swiveled 90° into the wing. "Hot" and "bouncy" on deck, the Corsair's most successful pilots were land-based Marines.

The Corsair was a quantum leap in fighter aircraft development and it soon endeared itself to all because it was a match for the Zero, but there were teething problems to overcome. Maj. J. Hunter Reinberg recalls, "To retract the wheels, a pilot had to be comfortably airborne before ducking his head under the instrument panel to reach the unlocking knob. If a pilot wore winged shoes, the shoe edge could catch under the locking knob and pull it out of the down lock detent. Occasionally, if he excessively seesawed the rudder pedals back and forth it inadvertently retracted the landing gear. Result: a bent prop, skinned-up belly, flaps worn off at their trailing edge and a verbal beating from the CO. An elongated fuselage forward of the cockpit housed a 237-gallon, multiple wall, self-sealing fuel tank which earned the aircraft the nickname 'Hosenose'. Obstruction to vision was especially bad for night take-offs and landings; no matter how a pilot sat, he just couldn't see over the nose."

Sunset in the Pacific and the propeller blades deservedly take a rest. The engine did pose problems at first: "The Corsair was our newest type fighter airplane, just completing its fourth month of combat. The engine was new and the most powerful yet built, but we had a number of mysterious high-altitude engine failures. We felt sure these were caused by unwarranted spark-arcing within the unpressurized magnetos while flying in the rarefied upper air, but in the meantime the war had to go on . . ."

A Corsair's wing guns receive their 2,350 rounds. These were used against Zeros to deadly effect by pilots like Maj. Reinburg: "My leading-edge machine guns spat flame as he exchanged lead with me. My tracers struck his airplane in the engine, and since every third bullet fired was a tracer, I knew he was getting hit thrice per tracer flash. Before completing a hard left turn, I was in firing position to kill another Zero. My cone of fire blew him up with a two-second burst."

Diving rocket attacks by the Corsair unnerved Japanese defenders on the occupied islands of the Pacific. F4U-1Ds and most subsequent models carried two 154-gallon (583l) drop tanks or two 1,000lb (454kg) bombs on twin pylons under the wings, or a 160-gallon (606l) drop tank and eight High Velocity Aircraft Rockets (HVAR) with 5in warheads. In 1944 fighter and dive bombing raids were increasingly carried out by US Navy VBF (fighter-bomber) and USMC squadrons in the ground-support role.

In November 1944 Hunter Reinburg led his squadron of Corsairs off from Peleliu atoll in the Palau Island group on bombing missions against by-passed Japanese-held islands, like Ulithi, Woleai and Yap, and to provide air defense for the US ground forces. Each plane carried one 500lb (227kg) general purpose bomb with an instantaneous nose fuze and a one-second delay tail fuze. Instructions were to, "Throw a 500lb GP on Yap as they passed", and strafe anything which seemed to need it.

Reinburg recounted, "We hit Yap right on the button after flying 262 miles over open water. The AA was already spitting in the sky as we rolled over for vertical dives. It was disgustingly easy to ascertain that there were no new targets, so I laid the egg on one of the AA positions and radioed my pilots to do likewise . . . My dive bombing pull out was made over the water." Pilots returned and bombed up again and again to hit targets in what became known as "Commuter Air Attacks".

TBF/TBM Avenger

"The TBF, the Avenger, was the first plane I flew on the Rudyerd Bay. When I sat in that airplane the first time, I wrote my parents to tell them that it's like sitting on top of a hay wagon loaded with hay. How on earth was I going to get that thing into the air? Actually, sitting up there was one of the great things about the TBF. You could look over the nose of the plane. It sloped down like a Saab automobile. The TBF was a lovely airplane. But it was, however, a heavy ship; and if you got over 150 knots, say up around 180, you would have to put both hands on the stick. The pressures were so heavy."

Gerrit H. Roelofs' impressions of the plane live in his memory. Despite the Avenger's less than successful debut in the Battle of Midway on 4 June 1942, when five of the six land-based TBF-1s of VT-8 (USMC) which had attacked the Japanese carriers were shot down into the sea, the fat bodied "Turkey" equipped all carrier based torpedo squadrons by the beginning of the Guadalcanal campaign on 7 August. Destined to become the Navy's leading torpedo bomber of the war, every new fast carrier from 1943 on had an Avenger squadron and they took part in every major battle in the Pacific. Best remembered for its joint actions with dive bombers, TBMs helped sink both the *Musashi* and the *Yamamoto*, then the world's largest battleships. Some 9,839 Avengers were delivered during 1942-45 and many remained in service long after the war had finished.

The TBF at right carries Lt. (junior grade) George Bush's name in recognition of the former president's career as the youngest naval aviation pilot in World War II. An Avenger pilot carried a lot of responsibility: he released the 22in torpedo or 2,000lb (907kg) of bombs in the internal weapons bay, and fired a 0.30in caliber Browning fixed machine gun on the upper forward fuselage. From July 1943 TBF-1Cs introduced two 0.50in caliber forward firing wing guns and bulletproof glass in the turret.

This head-on view of the Avenger shows off the fat bodied midwing monoplane design, massive Wright radial and the long weapons bay which could house either a torpedo, four 500lb (227kg) bombs, four 325lb (147kg) depth charges, or added fuel. Avengers on convoy protection duty aboard escort carriers shared in the destruction of 49 U-boats in the mid-Atlantic and they were the first American aircraft to be fitted with 5in rockets, first using them to sink a U-boat on 11 January 1944.

Two Avengers reveal their formidable armament. TBM/TBFs though still fell prey to the enemy. On 24 Janaury 1944 Imperial Japanese Army pilot Hideaki Inayama spotted two: "I hastily checked my remaining fuel and gave chase at full throttle. At 1,500ft two Avengers were flying southwards, their leader trailing smoke. Sitting ducks! I carefully turned in behind them, concentrating on the damaged Avenger, which still had its bomb bay doors open. Probably his hydraulics had been damaged . . .

600yds . . . 500yds . . . suddenly its ball turret gunner opened fire. Red tracers slipped past my Shoki, but I held my fire . . . 200yds . . . Now I was flying in the wash of my quarry and bouncing around like a mad thing. Steadying the Shoki, I fired at point-blank distance. Bullets from my four 13mm guns ripped into the Avenger, its 'greenhouse' canopy bursting into fragments like leaves in a gale. Flames seared back from over the port wing root, and the Avenger rolled over onto its back."

Grumman Avengers had a crew of three, a team in fact, and the gunner's power-operated turret behind the pilot housed a single 0.50in caliber machine gun. Gerrit Roelofs remembered, "I had a gunner in the turret behind me and the radio man had a little area behind the bomb bay. There was a little door on the right side that he used to get in, and he had a bench that he could swing out to do his work on. His instruments, radar scope, and radio were all down there with him. The radar was very primitive and was only good for 15 miles, if it was working at all. He also had a stinger gun that pointed toward the rear of the plane, which was his battle position. The radio man also had access to the after end of the torpedo, so he could set the depth that it would run. If you were going after a big ship, a carrier or something like that, you'd want to set the torpedo to run at 20ft so it would hit below the armour plate. If you were going after a destroyer, you'd set it for 8ft."

Lt. James T. Bryan Jr, late of the USS *Yorktown*, talked with a Grumman engineer and asked him, "How did you guys get a torpedo into the Avenger?" "We used a concrete dummy torpedo and a large forklift truck," came the reply. "Did you ever give any thought to the fact that there are no forklift trucks on an aircraft carrier?" Despite such gripes the use of airborne torpedo power was invaluable in a theater of war where large naval actions were commonplace.

F6F Hellcat

"The Kamikaze were all gone now . . . We had sunk a destroyer and a tanker, wounded a cruiser and severely damaged a battleship. But I had no time to ponder our success. The Hayabusa ahead of me waggled its wings in warning. A flock of Grummans was preparing to pounce on us. I had seen them streaking from the carrier – hornets angered at having their nests disturbed. Then I had lost track of them in the melee. Now, swiftly, two Hellcats were on my tail, 300yds off, firing bursts. Two more were moving up fast, maneuvering into firing position. Lead began to chew my stabilizer, and a 0.50in caliber slug pierced the canopy inches above my head . . . I executed an Immelmann, righting at the top of my loop just in time to see the Hellcat explode into nothingness . . .'

Gocho (Corporal) Yasuo Kuwahara was almost finally overwhelmed by sheer weight of numbers – five Hellcats tried to shoot the Hayabusa pilot into the sea – but a "divine storm" saved him; behind, two ships were missing from the American task force off Okinawa. The F6F had entered combat with VF-5 aboard USS *Yorktown* and VF-9 aboard USS *Essex* on 31 August 1943 and it immediately showed a marked superiority over Japanese aircraft. Hellcats were available in large numbers – by November 1945 some 12,275 F6Fs had been produced – and US Navy and USMC units claimed almost 75% of all air-to-air victories, with a ratio of 19:1. In the Battle of the Philippine Sea, 19/20 June 1944, Hellcats effectively halted the Japanese attack on the first day, accounting for most of the 300-plus aircraft shot down.

During the 19 June skirmishing seven F6F pilots each shot down five or more of the enemy. Lt. Alexander Vraciu of VF-16 on USS *Lexington*, the 24-year-old son of Romanian immigrants, shot down six "Judy" dive bombers to become, briefly, the US Navy's top ace with 18 victories. This restored F6F-5K was flown by Vraciu during training with VF-18 in the Hawaiian Islands. It is now repainted in the VF-6 markings during the time Vraciu notched nine "kills" flying from USS *Independence*.

Seated high on top of the fuel tanks the F6F pilot had superb all-round visibility, which he needed because the Grumman Hellcat had the largest wing area of any American single-engined combat fighter. Center-section pylons held either a long-range auxiliary fuel tank, which was jettisonable, or two 1,000lb (454kg) bombs. Underwing mountings could carry six 5in rockets or fuel tanks. Though it sports all his 19 "kills" (close-up, right), this Hellcat represents the F6F in which Lt. Vraciu scored 10 victories while serving with VF-16. Butch O'Hare had selected Vraciu as his wingman in August 1943 and the two became close friends, but that didn't mean O'Hare went easy on him. During training in Hawaii Vraciu had wanted to fly a P-40. O'Hare disapproved: "Why?" he asked. "Just so you can say you've flown one and look like a hot pilot?" He told his fliers that it was much more important to gain as many hours as possible in F6Fs, the planes they would fly in combat. Vraciu's record proves the point.

Apart from Vraciu and Harris, other aces such as Charles Mallory, Harvey Picken (11 victories each) and Robert Murray (10), all flew the F6F-5K Hellcat above, one of the most historic surviving F6Fs of the war, during their training. This particular Hellcat finished its training days in Vraciu's home town of Chicago where it equipped the Naval Air Technical Training Command and where, post-war, it was displayed at Wrigley Field. Restored, it is now based at Duxford, England.

The Hellcat looks mean and menacing. It duelled with Zeros right up to
the end of the war. On 29 March 1945 Roland Baker, VB-6, splashed one
Zero and looked for more: "Louis Davis went straight in. That awful sight
fixed my attention for that split moment but I came-to quickly as tracers
shot past followed by several hits opening up holes in the wing. I made a
tight left turn pulling Gs with the help of my G suit. Cherry Klingler,
division leader, shot the Zero off my tail."

Hellcat and Corsair, twin killers of Zeros in the Pacific war, commence their victory fly-by. By May 1945 F6Fs had destroyed 5,156 out of 9,282 aircraft shot down for the loss of only 270 Hellcats. Wildcats had held the line in the early days, but according to Charles Moutenot, of (VF)9 aboard USS *Essex*, "The Hellcat was a much better plane than the Wildcat but it didn't handle better . . . It couldn't turn as fast, for one thing. It was like going from a Chevy to a Cadillac."

Cadillacs of the sky had begun the rout in Japan 1944 when F6F units like VF-1 "Top Hatter" on USS *Yorktown* (above) so decimated the enemy that the action has passed into legend as the "Marianas Turkey Shoot." It was the beginning of the end: on 14 August 1945 the Japanese finally capitulated. On 2 September their swords were surrendered at a ceremony on the USS *Missouri* in Tokyo Bay. The Allies had finally laid to rest the cruel Empire of the Rising Sun. Unconditional surrender was theirs.

Boeing B-17G Flying Fortress

Type: Bomber with crew of six to 10.
Manufacturers: Boeing Aircraft; Douglas Corporation; Lockheed Vega.
Engines: Four 1,200hp Wright R-1820-97 Cyclones.
Dimensions: Span, 103ft 9in (31.6m); length, 74ft 4in (22.7m); height, 19ft 1in (5.8m).
Weights: Empty, 36,130lb (16,389kg); loaded, 55,000lb (25,948kg).
Performance: Max speed, 287mph (462kmh) at 25,000ft (7,620m); ceiling, 35,600ft (10,850m).
Armament: Thirteen 0.50in cal mgs; 12,800lb (5,800kg) bomb load.

Top: B-17E of 414th BS, 97th BG, used on the first 8th AF combat mission on 17 August 1942.

Bottom: B-17F of 322nd BS, 91st BG, lost on a mission to Stuttgart on 6 September 1943.

Consolidated Vultee B-24H/J Liberator

Type: Bomber with crew of eight to 10.
Manufacturers: Consolidated Vultee; Douglas Corporation; Ford Motor Co; North American Aviation.
Engines: Four Pratt & Whitney R-1830-65 Twin Wasps.
Dimensions: Span, 110ft (33.5m); length, 67ft 2in (20.47m); height, 18ft (5.49m).
Weights: Empty, 37,000lb (16,783kg); loaded, 65,000lb (29,484kg).
Performance: Max speed, 290mph (467kmh).
Armament: Ten 0.50in cal mgs; 8,800lb (4,000kg) bomb load.

Top: PB4Y-1 Liberator of PB Sqn VPB-110, US Navy, based at Dunkeswell, Devon, in the winter of 1944-45.

Bottom: Ex-389th BG, 8th AF, veteran B-24D Liberator "Little Gramper", 491st BG assembly ship, North Pickenham.

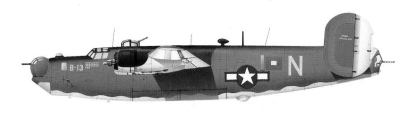

Boeing B-29 Superfortress

Type: Bomber with crew of 10.
Manufacturers: Boeing Aircraft; Bell; Glenn L. Martin Corporation.
Engines: Four 2,200hp Wright R-335-23 Duplex Cyclones.
Dimensions: Span, 141ft 3in (43.05m); length 99ft (30.2m); height, 29ft 7in (9.05m).
Weights: Empty, 74,500lb (33,795kg); loaded, 135,000lb (61,240kg)
Performance: Max speed, 357mph (574kmh) at 25,000ft (7,620m); ceiling 31,850ft (9,708m).
Armament: Eleven 0.50in mgs, one 37mm cannon; 20,000lb (9,070kg) load.

Top: B-29-45 "Enola Gay" of 393rd BS, 509th Composite Group, 315th BW, based on Tinian in 1945 and flown by Lt. Col. Paul Tibbets.

Bottom: B-29 (42-6242) tanker "Esso Express" of the 486th BG, XX BC, used to transport fuel to airbases in China.

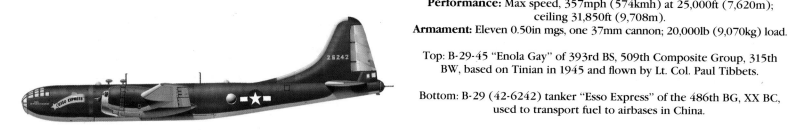

Lockheed P-38L Lightning

Type: Single-seat pursuit; long-range escort.
Manufacturers: Lockheed Aircraft; Consolidated Vultee.
Engines: 1,600hp Allison V-1710-111/113s.
Dimensions: Span, 52ft (15.85m); length, 37ft 10in
(11.53m); height, 12ft 10in (3.9m).
Weights: Empty, 12,700lb (5,760kg);
loaded, 21,600lb (9,798kg).
Performance: Max speed, 414mph (666kmh).
Armament: One 20mm cannon, four 0.50in cal mgs;
4,000lb (1,814kg) bomb load.

Top: P-38J of 338th FS, 55th FG, based at Nuthampstead,
England, in the spring of 1944.

Bottom: P-38J of 401st FS, 370th FG, based at Florennes, Belgium,
in November 1944.

Curtiss-Wright P-40N Warhawk

Type: Single-seat pursuit.
Manufacturer: Curtiss-Wright Corporation.
Engine: 1,200hp Allison V-1710-81/99/115.
Dimensions: Span, 37ft 3½in (11.36m); length, 33ft 4in
(10.14m); height, 12ft 4in (3.75m).
Weights: Empty, 6,700lb (3,039kg);
loaded, 11,400lb (5,170kg).
Performance: Max speed, 343mph (552kmh).
Armament: Six 0.50in cal mgs;
three 500lb (227kg) bombs.

Top: A gaily painted P-40E of 11th FS, 343rd FG, based in the
Aleutians in 1942.

Bottom: P-40 of the 3rd FS "Hells Angels" of the American Volunteer
Group (AVG) in Kunming, China, in the spring of 1942.

Republic P-47D Thunderbolt

Type: Single-seat fighter-bomber.
Manufacturers: Republic Aviation Corporation;
Curtiss-Wright Corporation.
Engine: 2,300hp Pratt & Whitney R-2800-59 Double Wasp.
Dimensions: Span, 40ft 9in (12.4m); length, 36ft 1in
(11.03m); height, 14ft 2in (4.3m).
Weights: Empty, 10,700lb (4,853kg);
loaded, 19,400lb (8,800kg).
Performance: Max speed, 428mph (689kmh).
Armament: Eight 0.50in cal mgs; 2,000lb (907kg) bomb load.

Top: P-47D-20 of the 19th FS, 218th FG, based on Saipan,
Marianas, in July 1944.

Bottom: P-47D of 86th FS, 79th FG, based at Fano, Italy, in
February 1945.

North American P-51D Mustang

Type: Fighter-bomber.
Manufacturer: North American Aviation.
Engine: 1,590hp Packard Merlin V-1650-7.
Dimensions: Span, 37ft 0½in (11.29m); length, 32ft 2½in (9.81m); height, 13ft 8in (4.1m).
Weights: Empty, 7,125lb (3,232kg); loaded, 11,600lb (5,262kg).
Performance: Max speed, 437mph (703kmh).
Armament: Six 0.50in cal mgs; 2,000lb (907kg) bomb load.

Top: Early P.51B assigned to 354th FG, 9th AF, for the tactical fighter-bomber role.

Bottom: P-51B of 318th FS, 325th FG, 15th AF, used in support of the Allied campaign in Italy, late in 1944.

North American B-25J Mitchell

Type: Medium bomber with crew of three to six.
Manufacturers: North American Aviation.
Engines: Two 1,850hp Wright R-2600-29 Double Cyclones.
Dimensions: Span, 67ft 7in (20.6m); length, 52ft 11in (16.1m); height, 15ft 9in (4.8m).
Weights: Empty, 21,100lb (9,571kg); loaded, 35,000lb (15,876kg).
Performance: Max speed, 275mph (443kmh).
Armament: Thirteen-18 0.50in cal mgs; 4,000lb (1,814kg) bomb load.

Top: B-25C-10 of 487th BS, 340th BG, based at Catania, Sicily, in September 1943.

Bottom: B-25C-20 of 81st BS, 12th BG, based at Gerbini, Sicily, in August 1943.

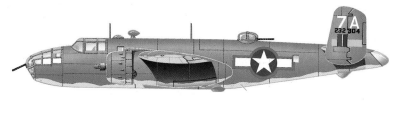

Martin B-26B Marauder

Type: Medium bomber with crew of seven.
Manufacturers: Glenn L. Martin Corporation.
Engines: Two 2,000hp Pratt & Whitney R-2800-43 Twin Wasps.
Dimensions: Span, 71ft (21.6m); length, 58ft 3in (17.8m); height, 19ft 10in (6.0m).
Weights: Empty, 23,000lb (10,433kg); loaded, 37,000lb (16,783kg).
Performance: Max speed, 310mph (500kmh).
Armament: Twelve 0.50in cal mgs; 4,000lb (1,814kg) bomb load.

Top: B-26G-1 of 456th BS, 323rd BG, based at Laon/Athies, France, during the winter of 1944-45 for night missions over Ardennes.

Bottom: B-26G-25 of 585th BS, 349th BG, based at Cambrai/Niergnives, France, in November 1944.

Douglas A-26B Invader

Type: Attack bomber with crew of seven.
Manufacturer: Douglas Corporation.
Engines: Two 2,000hp Pratt & Whitney R-2800-27 Double Wasps.
Dimensions: Span, 70ft (21.34m); length, 50ft (15.24m); height, 18ft 6in (5.64m).
Weights: Empty, 22,370lb (10,147kg); loaded, 35,000lb (15,876kg).
Performance: Max speed, 355mph (571kmh).
Armament: Ten 0.50in cal mgs; 4,000lb (1,814kg) bomb load.

Top: A-26B (44-34220) of 319th BG, 7th AF, based at Kadena, Okinawa, in July 1945 for attacks on Japanese airfields in China.

Bottom: A-26B (44-34323) of 3rd BG, 5th AF, based at San Jose on Mindoro in the Philippine Islands early in 1945.

Grumman F4F-4 Wildcat

Type: Single-seat, carrier-borne or shore-based, fighter.
Manufacturer: Grumman Aircraft.
Engine: Wright R-1830-86 Cyclone.
Dimensions: Span, 38ft (11.6m); length, 28ft 10in (8.5m); height, 11ft 11in (3.6m).
Weights: Empty, 4,900lb (2,222kg); loaded, 7,952lb (3,607kg).
Performance: Max speed, 318mph (512kmh).
Armament: Six 0.50in cal mgs; two 250lb (113kg) bombs.

Top: F4F-4 of VF-41 based aboard USS *Ranger* in early 1942. That May the rudder striping and the red disc within the insignia were erased.

Bottom: F4F-4 of VGF-29 with yellow insignia surround which signifies involvement in Operation Torch in November 1942.

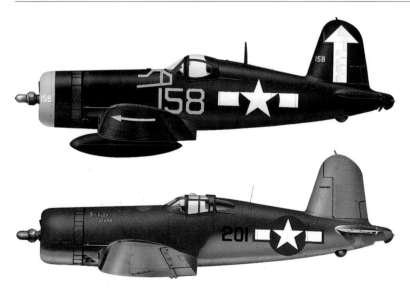

Vought F4U-1D Corsair

Type: Single-seat, carrier-borne or shore-based, fighter-bomber.
Manufacturer: United Aircraft Corporation (later Chance Vought Aircraft Inc).
Engine: 2,000hp Pratt & Whitney Double Wasp R-2800-8.
Dimensions: Span, 41ft (12.48m); length, 33ft 8¼in (10.27m); height, 14ft 9¼in (4.49m).
Weights: Empty, 9,900lb (4,490kg); loaded, 15,079lb (6,840kg).
Performance: Max speed, 395mph (635kmh).
Armament: Four 20mm cannon; two 1,000lb (454kg) bombs.

Top: F4U-1D of VF-84 aboard USS *Bunker Hill* in February 1945 when carrier aircraft took part in attacks on Japan.

F4U-2 night fighter of VMF (N)-532 USMC, based on Roi Island, Kwajalein Atoll, in 1944.

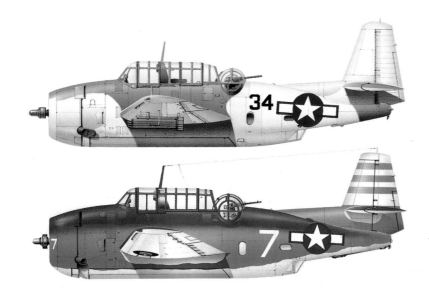

Grumman TBF/TBM Avenger

Type: Carrier-borne torpedo-bomber with crew of three.
Manufacturers: Grumman Aircraft; Eastern Aircraft.
Engine: 1,700hp Wright R-2600-8/20 Double Cyclone.
Dimensions: Span, 54ft 2in (16.5m); length, 40ft (12.2m);
height, 16ft 5in (5m).
Weights: Empty, 10,545lb (4,783kg);
loaded, 18,250lb (8,278kg).
Performance: Max speed, 267mph (430kmh).
Armament: Two 0.30in cal and one 0.50in cal mgs;
one 22in torpedo or 2,000lb (907kg) bomb load.

Top: TBF-1C of composite squadron VC-58 aboard USS *Guadalcanal*
on anti-U-boat operations in the Atlantic during spring 1944.

Bottom: TBM-3 serving with Task Force 58 aboard the USS *Randolph*
in the Pacific in 1945.

Grumman F6F-3 Hellcat

Type: Single-seat carrier-borne day/night fighter.
Manufacturer: Grumman Aircraft.
Engine: 2,200hp Pratt & Whitney R-2800-10W Double Wasp.
Dimensions: Span, 42ft 10in (13.0m); length, 33ft 7in
(10.2m); height, 13ft 1in (3.9m).
Weights: Empty, 9,042lb (4,101kg);
loaded, 12,186lb (5,528kg).
Performance: Max speed, 376mph (605kmh).
Armament: Six 0.50in cal mgs; six rockets; 2,000lb (907kg) bomb load.

Top: F6F-5N of the VF(N)-53, US Navy aboard USS *Saratoga*
during February 1945 when it saw action off Iwo Jima.

Bottom: F6F-3 of VF-16 aboard USS *Lexington* in September 1943
when it engaged in air operations against enemy-held Tarawa Atoll.

Note: All aircraft data featured is that for principal production models.

Acknowledgments
The publishers would like to thank the following organizations and individuals for their assistance in producing this book: Aviation Heritage: John Davidson, Jeff Ethell, Bradley Hood, and Charles Osborn; Cavanaugh Flight Center: Jim Cavanaugh and Sid Snedeker; The Collings Foundation: Jim Booth, Ned Bowers, Bill Clark, Joe Coleman, Bob Collings, Bobby Collings, Caroline Collings, David Frawley, Phil Haskell, Craig McBurney, Art McKinley, Jayson Owen, Mark Pinsky, Russ Pollina, Jonathan Rising, David Shepard, Steve Staples, Ted Stewart, and Gary Young; Confederate Air Force: Russ Anderson, Jerry Grizzle, Randall Sohn, and Barbi Woods; The Fighter Collection: Paul Bonhomme, Ken Fitzroy, Nick Grey, Stephen Grey,

Pete Kinsey, Hoof Proudfoot, and John Romain; Fighter Rebuilders: Kevin Eldridge and Steve Hinton; Flying Legend: Pascal Auchatraire, Franklin Devaux, and Christophe Jacquard; Imperial War Museum: Frank Crosby, David Henchie, and Carole Stern; Kentucky Aviation Museum: Norman Lewis; National Warplane Museum Geneseo: Bob Anderson; The Scandinavian Historic Flight: Lars Ness and Anders Saether; Sherman Aircraft Sales: Denise Sherman, Dennis Sherman, Kent Sherman, Patty Sherman, Scot Sherman, Sharon Sherman, and Terry Sherman; Warplanes International: Dick Foote; Weeks Air Museum: Linda Meyers and Kermit Weeks.

Thanks also, in alphabetical order, to the following people: James Bourke, Connie Bowlin, Edward Bowlin, Tony Buechler, Davina Bunce, Derek Bunce, Billy Burch, Selby Burch, Mel Cuslidge, Sebastien Dague, Larry Daudt, Bill Eagleson, Russ Harriman, Michael Heiny, Jonathan Lewis, Keith Mackey, David Marco, Pete McManus, Gary Norville, John Pitchforth, Rusty Restuccia, Terri Rodway, Joe Tobul, and Bob Tullius.

Photographic Credits
The black and white photographs were supplied by the author; others, where known, are copyright of the following institutions: **Page 39**, Smithsonian Institution 57890 AC. **Page 55**, USAF 300AC. **Page 67**, Smithsonian Institution 57886 AC. **Page 74**, USAF 60-21167. **Page 83**, RAF Museum P107010. **Page 101**, USAF 50192 AC **Page 105**, USAF 69813 AC. **Page 113**, Imperial War Museum FRA103030. **Page 119**, US Navy. **Page 125**, US Navy 95168. **Page 133**, US National Archives 80-G-43997. **Page 139**, US Navy 80-G-248440.

All the colour photographs in this book were taken by Patrick Bunce on Kodachrome film from Kodak UK, using Nikon cameras and lenses supplied by Nikon UK.